— THE —
UMBRELLA EFFECT

*A Journey of Self-Mastery
for Women Leaders*

ANA BARRETO

ISBN Hardcover: ISBN 979-8-9876158-7-4
ISBN Ebook: ISBN 979-8-9876158-9-8
ISBN Paperback: ISBN 979-8-9876158-8-1

Blue Hudson Group, Albany, NY

Books by Ana Barreto

Embrace Your Success: 8 Tools to Improve the Quality of Your Life
The Nine Powers of Women: Awakening the Divine Feminine Within
Women, Rice, and Beans: Discover Wisdom in Ordinary Moments
Self-Trust: A Healing Practice for Women Who Do Too Much
There is a Higher Power Within: 28 Meditation
Prompts to Find Peace & Happiness Within

Programs by Ana Barreto

Finding a Greater Wellbeing in a Busy World: Meditation
Discover Your Purpose & Mission
Clear Your Fear of Success
A Crash Course in Confidence
Timefulness: Making the Most of Life With the Time You Have
Nine Powers of Women Quantum Activation
Program - Healing Through the Chakras

How to connect online:

Visit http://www.ana-barreto.com for meditations,
classes, and inspirational content.
Like my page on Facebook: @ana1barreto
Follow me on Instagram: @ana1barreto
Follow me on Pinterest: @ana1barreto
Follow me on LinkedIn: anachavesbarreto
Send your comments, questions, and concerns to ana@ana-barreto.com

FREE GIFTS!

We have found that readers who download the free gifts mentioned throughout the book are able to take action and get results faster.

Ana-Barreto.com/Bonus

I dedicate this book to Laura, Nina, Ms. Alamina, and all the women who shared their stories with me so this book could grow wings.

CONTENTS

Introduction: Women with Purpose.................................xi
Chapter One: You Are Awesome!...1
Chapter Two: The Double Bind for Women Leaders................ 11
Chapter Three: The Costs of Ignoring the Self............................ 17
Chapter Four: The Top Three Behaviors Women
                     Must Change 27
Chapter Five: The Core Principles of Holistic Leadership 33
Chapter Six: Applying the Core Principles.................................. 39
Chapter Seven: The Body - Leadership Presence........................... 45
Chapter Eight: The Mind: Emotional Intelligence 55
Chapter Nine: The Spirit: Purpose and Meaning....................... 71
Chapter Ten: Stress Management and Self-Care 79
Chapter Eleven: Mastering the Basics (Management Skills)......... 95
Chapter Twelve: Your Values Are Your Compass 111
Chapter Thirteen: Confidence and Courage Matters...................... 121
Chapter Fourteen: Building Your Network of Support.................... 131
Chapter Fifteen: Fire Your Inner Saboteur...................................... 139
Chapter Sixteen: You Cannot Microwave Leadership 147
Chapter Seventeen: You Can't Teach Squirrels How to
                     Cross the Street...................................... 153
Chapter Eighteen: Leading as Your Whole, Authentic,
                     and Brilliant Self.. 159

Key Takeaways.. 163
Works Cited 165
About the Author.. 169

INTRODUCTION
WOMEN WITH PURPOSE

*"My mission in life is not merely to survive, but
to thrive; and to do so with some passion, some
compassion, some humor, and some style."*
— Maya Angelou.

S ome stories speak to the mind, but the best stories speak to the heart. Here is one of those stories.

The land was parched. For months on end, the sun blazed down, and there was not a single raindrop. The once lush green hills had faded to a lifeless brown, and the crops in the fields that fed mouths of all sizes withered under the relentless heat. As the village wells ran dry, a feeling of despair crept over the community.

Finally, a group of concerned elders approached their chief.

"Great chief," they implored, "we are in dire need of relief from this drought. Our livestock has begun to perish, and our children cry out from thirst. We beg you to guide us toward a solution."

The chief considered this, his fingers steepled under his chin, before replying, "This drought afflicts more than just our village. We must come together as a people and appeal to the heavens for rain through a sacred ceremony."

He designated the following Sunday as the day when the villagers would gather to pray, for this would allow even those working in the distant fields the opportunity to attend.

As the days passed, the anticipation grew. By Sunday, practically the whole village had converged under the Great Tree. They wore their finest traditional dress with bright colors in honor of both their chief and the skies from which they needed deliverance. They brought the best offerings they had. The villagers' rainbow dress contrasted with the pale dust that swirled around their feet. The chief arrived, adorned in intricately beaded lion pelts.

"Let us bow our heads and lift our voices to request relief from this merciless drought" his voice boomed out.

The villagers knelt reverently as they prayed for rain.

When the chief considered the kneeling crowd, he saw young Abeba, a girl not older than ten, holding an open umbrella over her head.

She was the only one who came fully prepared to receive the gift of grace. *That* is faith.

Our true feelings and beliefs are hidden in our actions, often unbeknownst to us. As you read this book, I urge you to bring your umbrella and expect a storm of changes.

Over more than thirty years of working with people in business, education, and their personal lives, I have met many amazing, talented women whose struggles may be familiar to you. They have found themselves afraid, tired, discouraged, and debating whether they should follow their career and ambition or settle for lesser roles. This has been an issue for hundreds of years.

Women have come a long way in leadership roles in business, politics, academia, and other spheres of influence at a cost that is too high for some. Not too long ago, they were not allowed to vote or to work after marriage. Yet, outdated gender biases and double standards still impose unfair expectations, criticisms, and discrimination on the gender.

For example, Margaret, a high-performer and dedicated young sales assistant who worked full-time while putting herself through college, was passed up for promotion right after getting engaged. Her manager assumed she would be distracted by the wedding plans, so an older woman was hired from outside the company to replace her.

Virginia, a standout manager who delivered excellent results across locations, exceeded in a rigorous interview process for a promotion. But when asked, she attributed her success to her "bubbly" personality. "Bubbly" was mocked by the executive to one of her managers. What did it even mean? The role went to a "not bubbly" man instead, whose results were less impressive than Virginia's.

Amanda, a bright young professional in her fourth year working in a not-for-profit role after finishing college, sat in an important meeting to discuss possibly renewing the contract with an outside contractor for another year. In the meeting, she shared with the team that the individual in consideration was sexist. Amanda described how this contractor constantly talked over her, ignored her input, addressed other employees next to her instead, and dropped the ball repeatedly, assuming she would pick up the slack. He wasn't pleasant to work with either. Another colleague confirmed Amanda's critiques were valid.

Despite this feedback, the group decided that the difficult male contractor was "coachable" and warranted renewing his contract for another year.

When Amanda returned to the office, her boss lashed out at her for making the "inappropriate" complaint about the contractor's sexism.

Her boss concluded his reprimand by saying, "When your personal life is in shambles, you bring it into the office."

He said this because Amanda's husband was hospitalized for four days for an autoimmune disease, while she kept working, seeming to suggest that even mentioning her troubles was a flaw. The boss chose to focus on Amanda's private life rather than the contractor's issues.

Christine was a veteran manager with over thirteen years of experience. She maintained excellent performance for a decade, becoming the go-to person for fixing performance issues and filling needed roles across locations.

Christine was successful despite not having full management training. Over the years, different senior leaders continually offered Christine promotions, yet she turned them all down. Finally, her boss's boss visited her office, urging Christine to accept a promotion. But instead, she requested to step down to a team member position! After watching the pressure her past bosses endured, she knew she didn't want to be a senior manager, even though she was fully capable and had already done some of the work required by the senior position.

Studies show that women in leadership often face a double bind where they are criticized for being either too soft or too aggressive. If they lead in a stereotypically feminine manner, they are dismissed as weak or emotional. But if they exhibit more authoritative traits, they are labeled bossy or called unpleasant names. This puts women in an impossible position where they cannot lead authentically without facing backlash.

It's time for women to become Holistic Leaders.

Holistic Leadership integrates the physical, mental, emotional, and spiritual dimensions of the self. It enables women to lead from a place of authenticity without leaving behind essential aspects of themselves. Primarily, Holistic Leadership teaches women that providing outstanding leadership doesn't come from stepping up, but by letting go of the thoughts and behaviors holding them back.

In this book, I will explore the common misconceptions women face, the frequent setbacks they experience, and successful remedies to help them own their brilliance and thrive in leadership as authentic, empowered, Holistic Leaders.

Why I wrote this book

After years of observing qualified women being overlooked, misunderstood, or more slowly promoted compared to male peers, I decided to stop complaining and take action. I had enough of being the only woman in the room and hearing my male peers remove women from the path to higher leadership. In 2018, I created a development program with support from Human Resources to advance high-potential women leaders in the company where I worked at the time.

We assembled a cohort of twenty-six accomplished women managers, recommended by their bosses, who were mostly male. Twenty-three women finished the program, and 65 percent of those were promoted within a year, even though some of the women needed convincing to take the promotion. It was good progress, but more was needed.

My research showed that women were promoted at less than half the rate of men. Many women have shared with me their frustrations and the need for development. Enough was enough.

Promotion Rates by Role Level for Men, Women, and Women of Color

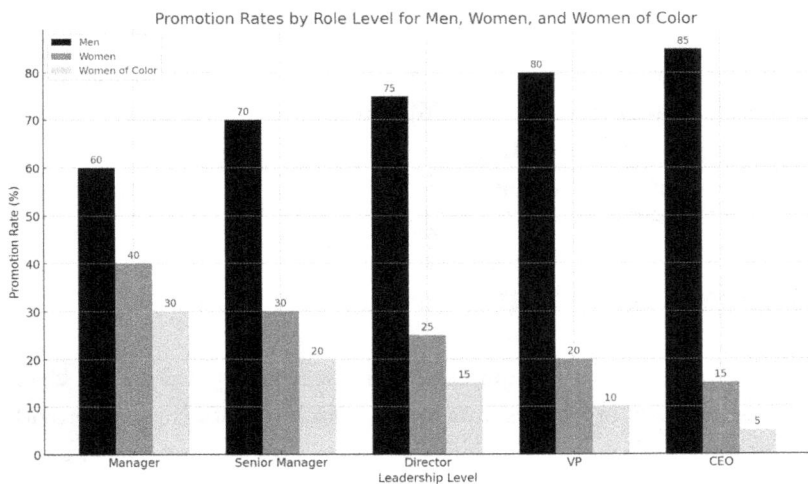

You possess a wellspring of inner wisdom. Often, outdated expectations can cloud it from view. This book guides you to look deep within and boldly bring your gifts into the world through your leadership at home, work, and in the community—no more fragmentation or self-doubt. The research-based framework and practices will help you align all aspects of your identity to shape an authentic Holistic Leader.

This book also provides the compass for the internal journey of owning your worth and arriving at your destination as yourself, and not what someone else thinks you should be. You'll master management fundamentals and reflect on your passions, strengths, values, and visions. You'll build emotional intelligence, mindfulness, stress resilience, and collaborative skills. You will learn the three most common mistakes women make in business and their personal lives, and learn how to correct them.

It's time to stop self-sabotaging and follow this Holistic approach to leadership—in behaviors (body), thoughts (mind), and meaning (spirit). This way, every woman knows that they deserve to own their seat at any table.

I compiled the knowledge and tools that are critical for women to lead with confidence into this book based on the program I created in 2018, the years working with women, my 30+ years of experience in the corporate setting, and research. You are about to read key lessons on becoming a brilliant Holistic Leader. Bring your umbrella.

The Journey Begins Within!

Defining Success and Fulfillment Holistically

Being a Holistic Leader requires defining success on your terms. Unexamined pursuits of titles, status, money, and validation rarely provide long-term satisfaction. Discover what matters to you, and find the path to achieve it.

Fulfillment flows from purpose-driven efforts, not a checklist of achievements. You'll learn to align your career with conviction, and see that work should fuel your spirit, not drain it. This holistic leadership, when applied strategically, creates ripple effects of influence, while energizing you from the inside out and expanding to other areas of your life.

I hope that by revealing the outdated biases and barriers that have long obstructed and discouraged qualified, talented women from advancing, we can dismantle them altogether. With the right skills and support, women can shatter glass ceilings and fulfill their immense potential as transformative leaders, without compromising their values and ambitions.

Ultimately, "The Holistic Leader" provides a blueprint for Leadership that allows women to leverage their strengths to lead brilliantly and authentically, without apology. The goal is to become more comfortable with your leadership style as you dissociate from poor role models and incorporate positive principles that fit your style and personal goals.

Your time is now. Journey on!

CHAPTER ONE

YOU ARE AWESOME!

*"The more you praise and celebrate your
life, the more there is in life to celebrate."*
— *Louise Hay*

The journey you are embarking on through this book requires curiosity, courage, commitment, and an umbrella. By dedicating reflective time to the practices in each chapter, you will unlock wisdom within yourself, new sources of confidence and influence, and a foundation for self-empowerment. Approach these moments as a transformational process.

To read this chapter, you only need one tool: *Your Breath.* You will need to breathe deeply, and even more deeply, whenever thoughts and emotions strike a chord. When we are upset, we tend to breathe shallowly to conserve energy. However, shallow breathing reduces the amount of oxygen to the brain, reducing our ability to think clearly. Your breath will help you remember who you truly are. Remember, your breath is a superpower. It will help reduce stress and see things clearly. Use it freely.

This chapter will guide you to reflect on your talents, strengths, growth areas, and passions so that you can lead authentically from a place of self-knowledge.

Know Yourself

The legendary philosopher Socrates said, "Know thyself." This simple but profound advice underpins all growth and fulfillment.

As a leader, understanding your natural strengths, weaknesses, motivations, and values allows you to operate from a place of authenticity and power. Lead from who you are, not who others think you should be.

Women, through no fault of their own, have created a persona they believed would better their lives. In business and personal life, behaving in a certain way would improve the odds of a woman getting her way. Pleasing the people around them and constantly assessing the environment to gauge reactions have resulted in too many women lacking self-awareness. They need to learn who they are, what they like, and what to do. Of course, not every woman falls into this category, but it won't hurt to investigate what percentage could be true for you.

Assess Your Strengths

During a coaching call, I asked a woman who planned to go back to work after raising children and caring for an elderly parent why anyone would hire her. What would she bring to the table? She didn't know. I have asked the same question of other women looking to be promoted, and they, too, struggle to answer. Regardless of your level in your career today, or lack thereof, start by making a list of your talents, skills, accomplishments, values, and passions. Pause now, get a journal, find twenty qualities about yourself, and write them down. Do not complete this work in your head. Do not wait until later. Use the margins of the book if needed. This is a foundation for a very important work.

Write down only your best qualities. Do not stop until you have twenty "gifts to the world" on the page. If negative qualities come to mind, toss them out. You have had generations of "putting women down" already. If you struggle to find your brilliance, let me suggest two items for your list. You have a heart that is capable of amazing things. It's beating now and inviting you to stay invested in your life. You have a brilliant mind that picked up this book to improve your life. You are supported by the talent of other women who came behind you so you can travel a unique path that no one else can take.

Once you have twenty (not nineteen!) qualities down, answer the following questions. It helps to play quiet music as you answer these questions. You can go to YouTube to find Theta Music.

- What comes naturally to you?
- What energizes you?
- When do you feel in flow?
- What are you proud of?
- How do others describe you?
- What makes people want to be in your company?
- What upsets you?
- When you were a child, what did you want to be when you grew up?
- Are you happy where you are in life today?
- What would you rather be doing?
- Write your heart out.

...

Once your fingers are done writing and your heart stops bleeding, stop and take three long breaths. Read the next three sentences slowly.

You are exactly where you should be.

You are exactly where you need to be.

This is a pause in your life to evaluate the destination, so when you arrive, you don't leave your true self behind.

If negative thoughts find their way into your head, don't let them rent space or squat. With each cleansing breath, you kick them out. In Chapter Four, you will learn how to remove such negative thinking.

Embrace Your Whole Self: Discovering Your Unique Gifts Through MBTI©

We each possess natural strengths and beautiful quirks that make us who we are. Gaining clarity on those abilities allows us to wield them more intentionally as leaders.

The first step in leadership is to understand who your natural self is. I like to use the Myers-Briggs Type Indicator (MBTI©) with my teams, which offers a framework for identifying personality preferences to understand and embrace your one-of-a-kind self.

First introduced by Carl Jung and then developed by mother-daughter duo; Isabel Myers and Katharine Briggs, MBTI© is a personality assessment tool that empowers self-discovery. It illuminates patterns in how you focus your attention, take in information, make decisions, and structure your life.

Every Leader's path starts with this kind of self-assessment. No ifs or buts. It's a non-negotiable to become a great leader and preclude the risk of being just a poor manager with a fancy title.

I like MBTI© because it's easy to access, with an online assessment that gives you great insights. You learn about your leadership style, decision-making, career path, communication, and how you manage change.

Chances are you may have taken MBTI© or other personality tests before. Often, when these tests are taken in a working setting, individuals tend to answer questions based on what they believe their employer wants them to be. This is a pity because all personalities bring something to the table.

There are no better or worse personality types, just different and equally valuable perspectives. Learning about personality through

MBTI© allows you to nurture your nature without judgment or comparison. You can lead with confidence by being your true self.

The Four Dichotomies of MBTI

MBTI© uses four dichotomies to classify personality into sixteen types. Each dichotomy reflects preferences between two poles:

Extroversion (E) – Introversion (I)

This scale measures whether you draw energy from the outer world of people and activity or the inner world of ideas and contemplation.

Extroverts are invigorated by social interaction and lose energy when isolated for too long. Introverts need solitary time to recharge before turning outward again. Based on the description above, do you find yourself more extroverted or introverted? Mark where you belong on the scale in the picture below. Neither pole is superior to the other, and the degree of introversion and extroversion fluctuates from time to time. At this time, where do you think you belong?

Extrovert ————————————————————————————————— Introvert

The balance between community and reflection serves everyone. Make space for what nourishes you.

Sensing (S) –INtuition (N)

This dichotomy indicates whether you tend to perceive tangible *details* or abstract *patterns* and meanings.

Sensors notice concrete facts and realities happening in the present moment. INtuitives focus on interpreting interconnections, symbolic meanings, and future possibilities. People who use the sensors as a preference tend to focus on details, facts, and proofs. People who focus on intuition tend to rely on insights with little additional information. Again, neither pole is superior to the other, and people tend to jump from one side of the scale to the other, but their preference defaults them to one side of the scale. Which side of the line do you spend more time on?

Sensing ————————————————|———————————————— INtuition

These modes of perceiving information are complementary. You can be open to fresh insights and novel imaginings without sacrificing pragmatism.

Thinking (T) – Feeling (F)

This scale reflects how you typically make decisions—through logical analysis, or based on values and social impact.

Thinkers excel at objectively assessing pros and cons to determine the most reasonable choice. **Feelers** shine at empathetically weighing how decisions affect others. **Thinkers** tend to follow one rule for all, while **Feelers** tend to adjust the rules to consider the impact level on different people.

Using the graph below, mark where you believe you default to it the most.

Thinking ————————————————|———————————————— Feeling

Logic and compassion together foster wise decisions. Blend reason with care, rather than suppressing feelings or avoiding softness.

Judging (J) – Perceiving (P)

This last dichotomy measures whether you tend to live in a more structured, decisive manner, or in a flexible, adaptable way.

Judgers thrive on planning, organization, and creating a sense of control. They dislike last-minute changes. Judgers are not about being judgmental but need order and planning in their environment. Perceivers prefer keeping options open and going with the flow. Perceivers shine in chaos. You can always spot the space between a judger and a perceiver.

Using the graph below, mark where you default to the most.

Judging ━━━━━━━━━━━━━━━┼━━━━━━━━━━━━━━■ Perceiving

Balance your scheduling with spontaneity. Structure provides stability, but flexibility allows growth.

Determining Your Type

You have self-assessed and identified the four letters representing preferences on each dichotomy. Now, write your MBTI© type below and remember them as I will refer to them often in this book. Use the highlighted area to identify your personality type letter.

━━━━━━━	━━━━━━━	━━━━━━━	━━━━━━━
Extrovert or Introvert	Sensing or INtuition	Thinking or Feeling	Judging or Perceiving

You might have been assessed previously by an employer or done one on your own for giggles. This time is different. First, you don't have the underlying pressure to share your full personality with your boss and portray the type of employee you think they will approve. Second, you can be 100 percent honest with yourself, because one of the intentions of a Holistic Leader is to be fully authentic. Third, you want to understand your default personality, the one who will show up when things fall apart.

Read the keywords for your personality below, and if you decide that you want a formal assessment, you can access it at Ana-Barreto. com/Bonus

ISTJ	ISFJ	INFJ	INTJ
Thorough	Conscientious	Insightful	Independent
ISTP	ISFP	INFP	INTP
Pragmatic	Low-key	Original	Analytical
ESTP	ESFP	ENFP	ENTP
Action Oriented	Enthusiastic	Charismatic	Adaptable
ESTJ	ESFJ	ENFJ	ENTJ
Logical	Cooperative	Supportive	Energetic

In life, every personality type brings something important to the table. If the world were composed of all extroverts, very few books would have been written. Important decisions would take forever if only sensing people were present. Every personality is needed to create balance, creativity, and growth.

Important Notes About Personality Assessment

- Some emotional conditions such as depression, being overwhelmed, and burnout can skew both formal and self-assessments.
- Around the age of forty, individuals begin to develop their opposite dichotomy. Extroverts become more introverted, thinkers become more feelers, sensing becomes more intuitive, perceivers become more judging and vice versa.
- A computer does not determine who you are; you do. You will need to be fully honest with yourself.
- People with high levels of any dichotomy tend to dislike people with high levels of their opposite.

When I began my MBA program, the entire class took the MBTI© assessment. We were divided into groups with different personalities and given an assignment to work on the entire semester. My MBTI© type is ENTJ. There was a student in my class that I didn't like very much, even though we had little contact until then. I didn't want that person on my team. She was ESFP. Because the Universe has growth lessons lined up for each of us, she became part of my team.

From the first meeting, I was annoyed with her. She slowed the group down, couldn't attend some of the meetings, and wanted to focus on issues that I didn't find important. As we got closer to the end of the class and had to present our thesis, I noticed that she had caught all of the mistakes we made. We did our presentation and then debriefed on the group dynamics.

We found out that from the beginning, we both didn't want to be on each other's team, for no valid reason. My teammate shared that she felt rushed by the group and believed we hadn't spent enough time on the thesis about performance evaluation. In the end, our group got an A for our thesis and an A+ for the team debriefing. We learned to appreciate each other's contributions. I valued the benefits of MBTI© assessments so much that later, I became a Certified MBTI© Facilitator and now use it in all my teams and coaching.

Now that you have identified your MBTI© type go to Ana-Barreto. com/Bonus to learn more about your personality. Use it for:

- Affirming strengths: What natural abilities can you develop?
- Building your Holistic Leadership skills: How can you use your strengths to become a better leader?
- Overcoming blind spots: What weaknesses need awareness?
- Understanding interactions: How do you connect with other types and create successful teams?
- Making empowered choices: How do options align with your nature?

Remember, MBTI© is for self-discovery, not boxing yourself in. Personality exists on a spectrum—be open to both preferences and appreciate your natural inclinations. Most importantly, embrace your personality as the wonderful gift it is as each type has its own beauty and brilliance.

CHAPTER TWO

THE DOUBLE BIND FOR WOMEN LEADERS

"You can waste your life drawing lines.
Or you can live your life crossing them."
— Shonda Rhimes

Women have made significant strides in reaching leadership positions across sectors like business, politics, education, and law. Yet, at the highest levels, from Fortune 500 CEOs to heads of state, leadership continues to be male-dominated. Women who do achieve top leadership roles find themselves in a double bind, facing contradictory expectations and no-win scenarios on account of gender bias.

Research has extensively documented this double bind. Studies show that women leaders are often criticized for being either too soft or too aggressive. They face backlash for exhibiting stereotypically feminine behaviors like cooperation and collaboration, but they also get penalized for displaying more authoritative, stereotypically masculine traits. This puts women in an impossible position where they are damned if they do and damned if they don't.

11

Damned for Being Too Soft or Damned for Being Too Aggressive

One horn of the double bind dictates that women leaders cannot be too feminine. Traits like nurturance, cooperation, and seeking input get interpreted as soft or weak leadership when displayed by women, but not men.

Within organizations, collaborative women leaders may be liked, but are not necessarily respected. Studies find that feminine or participatory leadership styles in women generate perceptions of weakness and indecisiveness among colleagues. This leads to their leadership capabilities and the potential for being underestimated.

Even when women exhibit the same behaviors as male leaders, they may be perceived differently. Identical actions are attributed to innate dispositions in women but situational factors in men. So assertive women seem abrasively "bossy" while assertive men just seem decisive.

On the other horn of the double bind, women get criticized for adopting the more stereotypically masculine behaviors necessary for leadership, like assertiveness, authoritativeness, and decisiveness.

Dominant, self-promoting behaviors often receive backlash when displayed by female leaders, who are seen as power-hungry or abrasive. Authoritative women are labeled bossy, aggressive, and unpleasant, even when engaging in the same behaviors as male colleagues.

One University of Arizona study demonstrated this clearly. Participants evaluated a company manager exhibiting dominant behavior without sharing their personal information. When they were told the manager's name was Brian, he was seen as significantly more likable and worthy of training than the identical manager named Karen.

Even famous female leaders fall victim to this bias. Hillary Clinton's strong leadership in her 2016 presidential run was often characterized as cold or abrasive. New Zealand Prime Minister, Jacinta Ardern gets painted as overly aggressive despite wide praise for her compassionate, holistic leadership approach during a crisis.

Psychological Impact of the Double Bind

Women leaders subjected to polarized feminine/masculine expectations report feeling psychological distress, anxiety about expected backlash, and confusion over how to lead authentically.

Trying to conform to contradictory expectations leads many women to second-guess themselves or suffer from impostor syndrome. It also contributes to burnout and turnover as women exhaust themselves while attempting to be perfect. They feel they have to work twice as hard as their male counterparts just to be acknowledged as leaders.

In fact, research shows that women leaders face heightened performance pressure. Mistakes they make tend to be judged more harshly than mistakes by male peers. Deficits in stereotypically masculine domains like strategic thinking or decisiveness draw harsh criticism. Women also tend to judge themselves as hard as their peers do.

Consider Katherine, who arrived two hours late for a meeting. She apologized and shared that she had written the wrong time down. Her boss ridiculed her in front of the group and picked on her for the rest of the conference, making inappropriate remarks such as, "Did you write this down?" in front of the group, even though she'd never been late before. In contrast, Mark, who was always late for conference calls and events, never received that kind of treatment.

Facing backlash causes many women to become risk averse, no matter what leadership style they adopt, and it pushes them away from pursuing higher-level leadership roles. Women end up opting out of advancement opportunities that could benefit their organizations and society.

Organizational Costs of the Double Bind

Discouraging women from bringing their full talents and leadership potential to bear has significant costs for organizations. Although no one will admit they are discouraging women from reaching their highest potential, it's happening everywhere through conscious and unconscious behaviors by both men and women. Pay attention to these statistics:

I. One in three women has contemplated downshifting their careers or leaving the workforce, compared to one in four who expressed this during the pandemic.

II. Four in ten women have considered leaving their company or switching jobs, and recent high employee turnover suggests that many of them are following through.

III. Fewer than half of women are satisfied with their current jobs, and 23 percent are actively considering leaving the workforce.

IV. One in four women is contemplating leaving the workforce or downshifting their careers, compared to one in five men.

V. 37 percent of women leaders have experienced a coworker taking credit for their ideas, and they are two times more likely to be mistaken for someone junior.

Women hold just 8 percent of top leadership positions in S&P 500 companies. That number drops even lower for women of color. The result is lost innovation, opportunities, and profit, all due to a lack of diversity.

Look to the woman on your right, then to your left, and see that at least one of you is in trouble. The time has come for every woman to carry an umbrella, and show the world around them how prepared they are.

Escaping the Double Bind

Clearly, organizations and society both suffer when women leaders feel forced to contort themselves to fit narrow gender expectations. The solution lies in taking a more holistic approach to leadership and extending the level of awareness of this unfair practice. It's time to educate the world.

Rather than viewing leadership traits as exclusively masculine or feminine, organizations must allow individuals to lead, leveraging their full range of capabilities. Leadership training, hiring practices, and culture must evolve to embrace inclusive models.

Women leaders, too, can learn to trust their own inner wisdom and lead from an authentic place of power. The following chapters will cover evidence-based techniques to help women maximize their strengths, manage expectations, and silence their inner critic.

By moving beyond restrictive feminine/masculine dichotomies, women can become more confident, holistic leaders. They can leave the pressure to inauthentically conform behind, and step into leadership. Not only does this benefit women themselves, but also their organizations and society as a whole. The tide is turning, but we must keep up the momentum.

CHAPTER THREE

THE COSTS OF IGNORING THE SELF

"It's not your job to like me - it's mine."
— Byron Katie

L et me reveal a hidden truth with the little tale of three women shopping for coffee.

A woman goes to buy coffee and finds only one wildly over-priced option at $1,200 a pack. Though exorbitant, she buys it because she really wants coffee, and money is no concern.

Woman B goes to another store with the same $1,200 coffee. She tries negotiating but only gets the price down a little, to $1,000, before caving. It's expensive, but she really wants her coffee.

Now, Woman C goes to yet another store and sees that same $1,200 coffee. She negotiates it down to $500 but decides even that is beyond her budget. Though she'd love the coffee, she walks away empty-handed, committed to drinking tea instead.

You see, when Woman A and B learn Woman C passed on the cof-fee despite getting it 50 percent off, they grow upset. They realize they overpaid relative to her deal. But the packages are already open—no returns or renegotiating now.

A and B feel trapped, having invested their precious time and money. Only now can they consider that perhaps C made the wise choice to walk away, though it seemed crazy to give up half-priced coffee!

The coffee represents your goals and ambitions, but you are not a commodity. When is the price of your success too much? Are you already paying too much for your success? As a Holistic Leader, you don't flee dreams, but align them with your heart. If they conflict, you're in the wrong place, and it's time to reset your inner compass.

Women attempting to adapt to the double bind of leadership often do so by minimizing or ignoring aspects of themselves. The statistics listed in the previous chapter showed that women would rather give up than fight what seems to be a losing battle.

When the multifaceted self gets suppressed or neglected, consequences arise emotionally, physically, and spiritually. Health suffers. Vitality wanes. Leadership presence diminishes, and meaning gets lost. This chapter explores the common costs women leaders face when parts of themselves get left behind.

Emotional Costs

Some people will be surprised that we are talking about emotional costs in a Leadership book. However, we can't talk about leadership without addressing its emotional impact on women.

Managing conflicting expectations and backlash takes an emotional toll on women leaders. Suppressing emotions like fear, vulnerability, sadness, or hurt requires immense energy. Putting on a mask at odds with one's true feelings breeds distress. Many women leaders end up feeling inauthentic, isolated, or burned out as a result. They want to leave, but when they have financial pressure to stay, that's what they do. They continue to work while yearning for something more.

Physical Cost and Burnout

Women experience burnout at approximately 1.5 times the rate of men. Pressure to consistently exceed expectations drives many to exhaustion. And ignoring personal and family life for work breeds resentment and emotional collapse.

In my book, *Self-Trust: A Healing Practice for Women Who Do Too Much*, I suggest that when women trust themselves, they stop overdoing and overthinking, and no longer feel overwhelmed, exhausted, or burned out.

Suppressing emotions and lacking support networks fuels burnout, too. Women who feel compelled to mute emotional needs like friendship, empathy, or work-life balance end up depleted.

Burnout impairs both leadership capacity and physical health. However, companies often overlook it until crises arise. Implementing flexible work policies, setting boundaries, and supporting resources reduce burnout risk proactively. However, organizations need to have the necessary conversations about the conscious and unconscious suppression of women in organizations.

Have you ever experienced burnout? When was the last time you felt overwhelmed, emotionally depleted, or exhausted? My research has shown that burnout is not a one-time incident, but a rollercoaster. People who experience this go through a cycle of being bored, overwhelmed, worn out, and finally burnout. Then, life makes them stop completely until they can recover, and the cycle starts again.

If you are falling into a pattern, I suggest a five-step program in my book *Self-Trust*.

- Step One – *Paying attention to what you do*. This will identify the behaviors that may seem unimportant but are depleting your energy and leading to burnout.
- Step Two – *Changing your mindset (thoughts, beliefs, and feelings)*. This will help you identify the internal thoughts that create the feelings and beliefs behind the actions that lead to burnout.

- Step Three – *Digging deeper.* This will go to the core wound that resides beneath the thoughts and beliefs that sabotage your intentions to live a better life.
- Step Four –*The Five Paths of Change.* This step will walk you through five stages to let go of past behaviors, with practical tools to build self-trust at a good pace so it becomes a habit.
- Step Five – *Sustaining changes.* This will help you with your long-term goals of living the life you want, without withdrawing your full participation in living life as you intended.

Burnout shows how people ignore their body's needs, damage their health, and diminish the energetic presence vital to influence. Yet, many women feel pressure to overlook their exhaustion, illness, or injury to prove themselves and serve others.

Impostor Syndrome

Impostor syndrome involves feeling like a fraud, the idea that one's success stems from luck or looks rather than qualifications. Women fall victim to impostor syndrome at nearly twice the rate of men.

Doubting oneself and working relentlessly to prove one's worth leads to anxiety, eroding the confidence necessary for leadership. For the women whose options are to stay on, when they see their inner criticism as irrational, the impostor syndrome diminishes.

When women feel like imposters, they attempt to fit rigid and unrealistic expectations they created for themselves, rather than expressing their true selves. One of the ways they try to overcome this is by mimicking masculine speech and behavior patterns that contradict their authentic personalities. This emotional incongruence undermines every unique and needed leadership capacity over time.

Lack of Self-Care

Good self-care habits like healthy food, exercise, sleep, and restorative practices reduce stress. However, many women leaders fail to prioritize self-care, believing leisure is lazy or indulgent. Violating the body's needs leads to depletion and long-term disease.

Some people think that they can function well with three or four hours of sleep, but they can't. Experts recommend that adults get between seven to nine hours of sleep per night for optimal health and performance. However, research shows people are sleeping less on average than decades prior, which comes at a cost.

According to a review in Sleep Health, adults sleeping fewer than seven hours nightly have elevated mortality risk. Short sleep duration is linked to an increased risk of diabetes, heart disease, obesity, depression, and motor vehicle accidents.

Making sleep a priority boosts motivation, mood, cognition, and overall well-being. Rest is essential, not a luxury. Building rest into schedules and routines sustains the energy needed to thrive. As Holistic Leaders, modeling healthy sleep habits also benefits their teams.

Women leaders can prioritize self-care in ways that enhance, rather than detract from, their leadership.

Methods of Self-Care

- Take brief five to ten-minute breaks each hour for meditation, stretching, or refocusing. Short breaks boost productivity more than working nonstop.
- Set boundaries around work hours, like not checking email after 7 pm. Create weekday evening and weekend time for rejuvenation. This has become much more important since the workforce has shifted to work from home and the separation of work and family life has blurred.

- Build regular movement into each day, even if it's just a walk around the office or doing yoga. Exercise reduces stress and boosts energy.
- Take regular vacations and sabbaticals to unwind and gain a broader perspective. Time away replenishes creativity and motivation. If you typically cash in some of your vacation time, stop it! No amount of money is worth the price of your well-being.
- Cultivate rewarding relationships outside of work, through community, socializing, family time, or volunteering. Supportive connections feed the soul.

Strategic self-care makes women more present, energized leaders. It models good work-life balance for colleagues as well. Intentionality, self-care, and strong leadership complement each other.

Spiritual Costs and Meaning

When my younger self arrived at my dream job of working in New York City as a Director of Sales and Marketing, a position I had set my eyes on only five years earlier, I couldn't foresee that living my dreams would make me so unhappy. Being the top-performing unit in the division didn't take away the misery I felt. It turns out that in the quest for external markers of success or financial endurance, women leaders may lose connection to their inner wisdom, ethics, and purpose. Ignoring their inner compass for status or survival leaves them rudderless.

When work focuses solely on status, profit, and achievement, its meaning gets lost. Women who suppress values and passions to fit the expected leader archetype often end up disillusioned.

It's important to cultivate purpose, and aligning work with beliefs is vital for fulfillment. Leaders should assess whether pursuits honor their deepest commitments. What is success worth if it's not guided by wisdom?

What is Your Definition of *SUCCESS*?

For some people, success is making lots of money. For others, it is having a large family. For a few, it's a position as CEO. What is *your* definition of success? If you silence all of the expectations placed on you, imposed or not, where do you want your path to lead?

Please note that I said "path." Success is not the destination. This is one of the biggest misconceptions that career-oriented people have. Success is the way. Success starts when you wake up each morning, with how many times you snooze the alarm, and how you enjoy your shower to motivate you or shake off the day. Success commutes with you to work and spreads through your office, meetings, and Zoom calls. Success travels with you and socializes in the cafeteria. Success is not a forty-year retirement plan; it's now.

Take your journal and answer the three questions below to help you gain clarity about your success. Be bold and creative, and imagine every aspect of your vision of success.

Tune into your unique passions to set meaningful goals. Your vision needs to feel inspired, not imposed. Imagine your best self, living your best life.Take the time to imagine and then answer the Three Questions below.

Three Questions:

- What experiences do you want to have in your life?
- How do you want to grow?
- How do you want to contribute to the world?

You can download a form to complete these questions at Ana-Barreto.com/Bonus.

This form is meant to be posted on your office walls, bedroom walls, or bathroom mirror so you can see it often. It will help you redesign your life with your newfound definition of Success.

Please don't do it in your head. Writing it down helps you recall and activate multiple areas of the brain that will guide you to achieve your goals. Professor Gail Matthews from the Dominican University in California found that by writing down your goals, you are 42 percent more likely to achieve your definition of success.

You Have Choices

Now that you have an unfiltered definition of success, what is holding you back? Every moment you stand at a crossroads between many possibilities and your comfort zone, you waste your talents. Not choosing is a choice, and you need to choose consciously. Choosing growth and contribution over complacency is the path to becoming the type of Holistic Leader everyone wants to follow. If you've decided that your current path isn't working, keep reading, because your talents and leadership will be needed wherever you go.

Holistic Leadership reminds you that you possess innate wisdom. Like a sun behind clouds, a wise inner voice speaks within you, however softly at times. It holds your truths, desires, and highest potential, if you listen. Still, you have a choice: will you listen, or ignore it?

Leadership begins by choosing to trust your inner wisdom over doubt. Self-belief seems risky only because it contradicts past notions that you must wait on others' permission or validation. Women were taught by generations to be seen and not heard, to play small, to not ruffle any feathers, and to do as they're told. We all know that this is intrinsically wrong on so many levels.

Today, you are validated by your inner guidance to become the Holistic Leader at work, home, and community. The choice to honor your inner knowing is the first step.

Every moment, we choose, consciously or not, to be comfortable or courageous. As Eleanor Roosevelt said, "No one can make you feel inferior without your consent." Blaming women's history, circumstances, upbringing, and the past is soul-depleting. The empowered choice you are called to make is to determine, from here forward, how you will think, feel, act, and become the woman you want to be by your own standards.

You answered those three questions above, which gave you some clarity. Read your answers. Reflect on them and make wise decisions.

A Holistic leader challenges limited perspectives. Here are some reflective questions for you to ponder. Again, write your answers in your journal.

- What limiting beliefs are in the way of you making a decision?
- What habits need to be renegotiated so you can make the choices that are right for you?
- What decisions do you need to make but are afraid of and why?
- Who used to make decisions for you?
- Do you have to tiptoe around someone about the decisions you need to make?

Perhaps this is the time to leave the easy ways behind and play big. It doesn't have to be today. Today, you just need a decision. I learned that when a thought keeps coming back around, it's time to take action on it. Every action starts with a decision, and your choices will create ripples.

CHAPTER FOUR

THE TOP THREE BEHAVIORS WOMEN MUST CHANGE

"We need to accept that we won't always make
the right decisions, that we'll screw up royally
sometimes - understanding that failure is not
the opposite of success, it's part of success."
— *Arianna Huffington, Author*

Part of your awesomeness is your unique ability to envision the future. Every moment you create starts with a vision. That vision creates your life. If you don't like your life, change the way you envision it, or you will continue to live your life on default.

In the last chapter, you were called to make a decision. Once you do that, it's time to envision. If you envision being a great leader and taking your career to the next level, here are the Three Behaviors Women Must Change today:

Behavior #1: Expecting the Worst

Many women scare themselves from doing anything by imagining the worst-case scenario. I used to do it, too. Now, it's time to stop!

Those negative thoughts are leading your attention to the things you don't want instead of the outcomes you do want. Look in the mirror and check if you have been a "Negative Nelly." There is no "Negative Neil," only a Nelly. If your attention habitually gravitates toward catastrophes, you can do something about it.

The need to imagine disaster is a trick of the mind to stop you from going forward, protect you from getting hurt, and prepare your emotions for disappointment. This just sets you up to accept failure. Your emotions are leading the way down to insignificance.

How about envisioning the best outcome? What if you win big? What if you get the recognition, the promotion, the money, the partner, the life beyond your expectations? How would you feel when amazing things happen? Think about it. Then, feel how you would feel when the best scenario happens. That's the emotion to unlearn the old pattern of sabotage.

Every time you find yourself imagining the worst, stop and say out loud, "I don't want this. This is what I want," and say what you want to happen instead. This is simple, but it works. It will take lots of repetition until you master it. I know it because I used to be there.

Your life will reflect your uniqueness when you display it in the world. Practice it. Envision the best coming your way. Imagine yourself leading boldly from wholeness and conviction, meeting your definition of success. Let this vision pull you forward.

Behavior # 2: Stop Minimizing Yourself

Many women have been socially conditioned to preface their ideas by minimizing themselves. How often have you started to share a thought in a group or meeting by saying, "I'm sorry, but…" or "This may be a silly idea, but...."? We unwittingly sabotage our contributions in advance by framing them through apologies and disclaimers.

Starting sentences with "I'm sorry" instantly disempowers whatever we say next. It casts our perspectives as inferior or inadequate before anyone even hears them. The reflex comes from a place of being unable or unwilling to own our worth and voice. True leadership requires confidently sharing ideas without undercutting them at the outset.

Next time you feel compelled to apologize before presenting an opinion, stop yourself. Take a breath and rewrite the script in your mind. "I have a perspective to share on this problem that may help us find solutions." You have valuable wisdom to contribute. Discard pointless apologies and stand proudly in your worth. Let your ideas speak for themselves, without self-imposed diminishment. You deserve to take up space and be heard.

Until you can say your thoughts with full confidence, you can say, "Mark, in my experience, (share your thought)" or "Tom, here is another way to look at it (share your opinion.)

Always use the name of the person you are addressing. People like hearing their names and are thus more likely to pay full attention to you.

Behavior #3: Silencing Your Voice

Far too often, women bite their tongues when they have something to say in meetings or group settings. We hesitate to interrupt or speak up quickly, even if we have urgent insights to share, so we miss the chance to contribute meaningfully.

This tendency to minimize ourselves by waiting and staying silent is a learned behavior. As little girls, we got scolded for being "too loud" or "speaking out of turn." Now, we police ourselves by lingering in silence, even when we have the answers. Sometimes, women passively wait for impossibly perfect timing, until someone else says what they want to say, preempting their idea.

During one of the Women's Development trainings, a manager shared that she always hesitated to speak when the boss asked questions. Then, her coworker shared her idea, which she had shared with her peers. She was so upset that she left the meeting immediately to cry in the car. The ideal solution to prevent experiences like this is to speak up and share your ideas first. When someone else shares your idea for you, be ready to address the issue and take credit. Please, *do not* yell out loud that it was your idea! Instead, say gracefully, "Hey Tom, Mark is right. When I came up with this plan and implemented it before sharing it with everyone to ensure it would work, I met with these outcomes ..."

I have been in meetings where no one knew the answer to the boss's questions, and everyone stayed silent until I voiced it out. It turned out that none of the boys would admit to not knowing. However, true confidence requires you to own your position. You can start saying something like, "*I may have missed it, but I don't recall reading that.*"

In calls with my teams, many of the women would wait until the call was over to ask me a question. Other times, they texted me questions during the call. They were valid questions, and I am sure others needed the answers, too. Why would anyone be afraid of asking questions? Perhaps they have been shamed for not knowing the answer in the past, or they were embarrassed for not knowing the answer, or just wanted to keep up the persona of knowing all.

Any leader who shames someone for asking a question the leader assumes they should know must be fired. Holistic Leaders encourage questions to ensure others have the tools and knowledge to complete the job and win.

As leaders, we must unlearn old patterns and practice confidently voicing perspectives, asking questions, and steering conversation. Do not overthink it or rehearse it in your head for too long. If you have something meaningful to contribute, speak bravely when moved to. You add immense value through your lens.

Take Action

This is your moment. You know the path and are open to successful outcomes. You know your natural and dormant talents. You made a decision and can envision the outcome. Now, take small steps toward it.

What are the steps to take?

A Holistic Leader takes action. Pull out your journal and write the actions you need to take. Don't worry about *how* you are going to do them, just write them down—no need to put them in order or check the spelling. If you are a MBTI© Sensing, be mindful that too many details may derail you from the creation process. You want it to flow. Take at least ten minutes to write everything you need to do.

Go back to your three questions. Please read them. Now, use your list to validate whether the actions you wrote down are aligned with your goals. For example, if you envision making more money, you may need to ask for a raise, perform better, or change jobs. Having a conversation with your boss, updating your resume, or getting your team to be enthusiastic about their job could be important steps.

Action creates opportunity, releases stagnancy, and breeds courage. So, choose one small action to take. You know you want to go to another level, or you wouldn't be reading this book. When you take consistent action, confidence grows. New choices become conceivable, then achievable.

CHAPTER FIVE

THE CORE PRINCIPLES OF HOLISTIC LEADERSHIP

*"The question isn't who's going to let
me; it's who is going to stop me."*
— Ayn Rand

I t's not surprising that mainstream leadership theory evolved from male-centric perspectives. The ideal leader is often portrayed as aggressive, competitive, authoritarian, and dynamic. This leaves little room for stereotypically feminine traits like cooperation, nurturing, and vulnerability.

Though often discounted as touchy-feely, qualities like emotional intelligence, communication, collaboration, and empathy strongly predict leadership effectiveness. A large-scale study by research firm Zenger Folkman explored the impact of "soft" leadership behaviors.

They found a significant positive correlation between traits like building relationships, inspiration, self-development, and overall leadership success. Leaders who exhibited these strengths were far more effective at driving results, engaging teams, and building trust.

Many Ivy League schools and other top universities recognize the importance of developing strong soft skills, and now offer classes focused on improving emotional intelligence, communication, collaboration, and more. Yale University offers courses for improving interpersonal skills, like "The Science of Well-Being," which teaches students strategies derived from positive psychology research. They also offer classes on mindfulness, resilience, leadership, and more.

Hard data substantiates the immense impact of soft skills on leadership excellence. Social-emotional abilities provide a competitive edge. Leading with compassion and emotional wisdom achieves results while also uplifting people.

The workforce today calls for more Holistic models of Leadership that embrace feminine energy and offer paths for more impactful and authentic leadership. Instead of trying to fit a square peg in a round hole, how about using the round peg representing 50 percent of the population, women, who are ready to fit into the round hole of leadership?

Rise of Transformational Leadership

James MacGregor Burns originated the concept of transforming leadership in his Pulitzer Prize-winning 1978 book *Leadership*. Unlike transactional leaders who use carrots and sticks, transforming leaders connect work to values and higher purpose.

Transformational Leadership focuses on:

- Inspiring vision and shared goals
- Stimulating innovation and problem-solving
- Developing potential in individuals
- Promoting collaborative cultures

This approach championed stereotypically feminine behaviors like participative decision-making, mentoring, and elevating others' needs. Subsequent research confirmed its advantages. Transformational Leadership correlated strongly with team cohesion, job satisfaction, reduced stress, and better financial outcomes.

Bernard Bass further developed the model, differentiating transformational from transactional approaches. He highlighted four components of transformational leadership:

1. *Idealized Influence* – Serving as an ethical role model
2. *Inspirational Motivation* – Articulating a compelling vision
3. *Intellectual Stimulation* – Encouraging innovative thinking
4. *Individualized Consideration* – Developing others via mentorship

These four pillars exemplify Holistic Leadership, integrating masculine and feminine strengths. They offer women pathways to lead powerfully in their own right.

Holistic Leadership

Holistic Leadership has its foundation in Bass's updated Transformational Leadership and purposefully integrates multiple aspects of self. It engages the mind, body, spirit, and heart in service to the mission and the people, including oneself.

Rather than viewing traits as gendered, Holistic Leadership highlights strengths from all quadrants of being (mental, physical, spiritual, and emotional), and externalizes wisdom accumulated through diverse life experiences.

Holistic Leaders flexibly shift between leading and following, as needed. They build collaborative relationships grounded in ethics. Instead of control, their power stems from serving, integrity, inspiration, and interdependence.

This framework allows women to lead authentically without adopting distorted masculinized behaviors. They can leverage feminine energies alongside reason and strength.

Core Principles

Holistic leadership aligns with values, purpose, and authentic self-expression. It fosters development in self and others.

The Core Principles include:

1. Integrating intuitive, emotional, and rational ways of knowing
2. Promoting ethics, integrity, and social responsibility
3. Cultivating mindfulness, self-care, and continuous growth
4. Facilitating participation, power-sharing, and "leading from behind"
5. Tapping interconnectedness and interdependence for collective wisdom
6. Allowing vulnerability and humanity to build trust and resonance

This approach provides women space to lead from their strengths. The following chapters explore holistic leadership practices in more depth.

By expanding beyond the narrow traditional leadership ideal, women can access their full capabilities. They can lead while being integrated, energized, and true to themselves, revolutionizing organizations, communities, and lives in the process. The Age of Holistic Leadership is dawning.

Debunking "Survival of the Fittest"

As I write this book in 2023, I hear top thought leaders still talking about survival by competition, and how women's nature is oriented around competition. One of these individuals shared his view that when women synchronize their periods, this is a natural way to eliminate competition.

This archaic and erroneous male perception can be explained by the years of indoctrination of the male point of view. The notion that humans must compete and be cutthroat to survive stems from a flawed interpretation of Darwin's theory. "Survival of the Fittest" was meant to explain natural selection, not justify ruthlessness.

New research has debunked the poor interpretation of Darwin's theory in the business arena. In fact, cooperation, not domination, is what has enabled humans to evolve and thrive. Shared intelligence, group protection, and division of labor is what allows communities to flourish.

Leadership that supports collective survival outperforms autocratic control. As mammals herd, ants swarm, and geese fly in a V, there is wisdom in numbers among humans as well.

Cooperation draws on feminine energies of building rapport, elevating others, and seeking shared goals. All of this together power transformation.

When women spend time together and synchronize their periods, they are not out to eliminate competition but to share their time in the community and the wisdom those days provide. In ancient times, women would create a circle and spend their time of the month in a hut. They were not impure, as some cultures proclaimed. They sang, shared stories, cried, received guidance, and provided support for each other. Mostly, women were allowed to have downtime. The tribe immensely valued those days. Often, other tribe members would consult the women for their wisdom immediately after the hut time was over.

Survival through partnership represents the best of human nature. Cooperation, not competition, drives positive change.

CHAPTER SIX

APPLYING THE CORE PRINCIPLES

"Self-awareness and self-love matter.
Who we are is how we lead."
— Brené Brown, Author

The 6 Principles of Holistic Leadership

The 6 Principles of Holistic Leadership provide a comprehensive framework for effective and ethical leadership in today's complex world. These principles go beyond traditional leadership approaches by emphasizing the importance of considering the whole system, fostering collaboration, and making decisions that benefit all stakeholders. By embracing these holistic principles, leaders can navigate challenges with greater wisdom, build trust and buy-in, and create positive change that resonates across their organizations and communities. In the following sections, we will explore each of the six principles in depth, offering insights and practical guidance for embodying a holistic approach to leadership.

Principle 1: Integrating intuitive, emotional, and rational ways of knowing

This means tapping into multiple facets of knowledge to inform leadership. Rather than relying solely on cold, hard facts and data, Holistic Leaders also tune into their personal instincts, emotions, and intuitions when making decisions and relating to others. They believe important truths can be found through diverse paths of understanding. This method is used often, but needs to be more widely recognized and validated.

Every time someone acts on a hunch and gives an opportunity to someone who would be fired, or adjusts a company's standards to meet their people's satisfaction, they are acting on the first principle of Holistic Leadership.

I used to ask my managers what they would do in this scenario. But first, I assured them there was no wrong answer: If an employee didn't show up to work, didn't call, and returned two days later saying her mother died, would you give her a final write-up or just let her off the hook? What would *you* do?

Fifty percent of my managers would write her up, and the other fifty would overlook the incident. One of my male managers even said, "I would write her up, and I would ask her if her phone died, too." Needless to say, most of my managers who would write her up are logical MBTI© Thinkers. In the past, they wrote up everyone who didn't call and didn't show up to work. The managers who let it go were mostly MBTI© Feelers. They felt tremendous empathy for the employee and imagined how they would feel if their own mother died. Also, I suspect that some of the managers answered the question trying to consider how I would like them to answer.

This principle calls for Holistic Leaders to be balanced decision-makers. There is no wrong approach here. If **T**hinking leaders decide to write her up, or **F**eeling leaders decide to give her a pass, they are both right by following their natural inclination and the culture of the organization. The balanced action for a Holistic Leader is to find the right time to exercise the disciplinary action or follow up conversation. Immediately is not always the right time.

Principle 2: Promoting ethics, integrity, and social responsibility

Promoting ethics, integrity, and social responsibility involves leading by example to foster an ethical organizational culture. Holistic Leaders hold themselves and others accountable to moral principles and serving the greater good. They seek to align organizational values and practices with ethical codes that respect human dignity, environmental sustainability, and social justice.

During the Black Lives Matter Movement, many companies made the decision not to allow employees to wear promotional items supporting the cause, while others did allow it. Some cases went to court. Without a political agenda, racial profiling and discrimination were at the forefront of the news. Companies cannot ignore the sense of integrity and social responsibility. You cannot be "Switzerland"; you must commit to a side.

Principle 3: Cultivating mindfulness, self-care, and continuous growth

Cultivating mindfulness, self-care, and continuous growth emphasizes leadership that starts from within. Holistic Leaders commit to developing self-awareness, managing stress, and expanding personal capacities through reflective practices like meditation, journaling, walking in green spaces, and practicing yoga, tai chi, or qigong. By taking responsibility for their own health and growth, they are better able to serve others from a place of wholeness.

Miserable leaders create hostile environments. I had a leader who would sometimes walk into work and say hello to everyone he encountered on the way to the office. Other days, he was so unhappy with life that he didn't say hello to anyone and made his way to the office as quickly as possible. Those days, the team members would text each other to stay away from the boss.

I had a conversation with that manager, who shared that he had five children, had a fight with his wife, and needed to make more money. A Holistic Leader doesn't have to be happy 24/7, but they need to manage their emotions. One of the strategies Holistic Leaders can use when bad things happen is to connect with gratitude.

On the bad days, when the world is collapsing, find twenty things about your job or life to be grateful for. In five minutes, you can improve your personal state, because you cannot be grateful and miserable or angry at the same time. It's impossible. The tricky part is finding the twenty things, especially when you are in the hole. If you can name twenty things now, when you are okay, you will be able to get there even when you are not at your best. This works amazingly well when you try it.

Principle 4: Facilitating participation, power-sharing, and "leading from behind"

Facilitating participation, power-sharing, and "leading from behind" means adopting an inclusive, collaborative leadership style. Rather than asserting top-down control, holistic leaders actively engage stakeholders, delegate authority, build teams, and support others in taking charge. They lead by empowering rather than wielding power over others.

Holistic Leaders serve others. Their job is to ensure everyone has everything they need to do their job, is happy at work, and feels successful.

Principle 5: Tapping interconnectedness and interdependence for collective wisdom

Tapping interconnectedness and interdependence for collective wisdom recognizes that no one leader has all the answers. Holistic leadership leverages the talents and perspectives of those across the organization and community. By fostering diversity and relationships, Holistic Leaders draw out synergistic solutions that emerge from a spirit of cooperation.

One strategy to bring this principle to life is to foster talents by assigning people to lead groups, meetings, and initiatives where they are happy to do it and will share their knowledge and wisdom across the organization.

Principle 6: Allowing vulnerability and humanity to build trust and resonance

This requires showing one's true self. Rather than putting on a facade of invincibility, holistic leaders reveal their authentic selves with transparency and humility. This fosters human-to-human bonds, empathy, and mutual understanding to unite people behind a shared purpose.

For many years, we were told to leave our home life outside of work. It was the rule of survival. Men are far better than women at compartmentalizing their lives and leaving their home life issues at the door. This is not how women function, and it's not healthy for men either.

Marcia found out that her husband was having an affair with someone she knew. She was devastated by it but didn't tell anyone or confront them. She kept it to herself for three days until, on her way to work, she had a stroke.

The lines between personal and work lives blur all the time. It's insensitive of leaders to ask others to forget or ignore their personal issues at work.

When my children were young, I couldn't concentrate at work if I felt they were not well. Not until I found the right childcare was I able to deliver better results at work. When they graduated pre-school, I cried, not for the special moment, but because of the immense gratitude I felt for the teachers and the facility. They were an integral part of my success.

I couldn't imagine managing my career and home life during the lockdown. The COVID-19 pandemic had a significant impact for women on the workforce. In the U.S. alone, 2.3 million women left the labor force due to childcare responsibilities, health concerns, and loses of jobs in the sectors dominated by female labor. For the women who stayed, they were often criticized for dividing their time between work and childcare. Some leaders expected them to choose the work over their children.

CHAPTER SEVEN

THE BODY - LEADERSHIP PRESENCE

"You are the only person who can use your ability."
— Zaha Hadid

B eyond skills and smarts, effective leaders exhibit an energetic charisma or "presence" that resonates with others. Leadership presence stems in large part from mindfulness of the physical body. This chapter explores how women leaders can cultivate presence by getting grounded in the body.

The Impact of Presence

Leadership presence creates contagious confidence. Composed, focused, and grounded leaders inspire trust and communicate vision powerfully.

Studies reveal that presence accounts for up to half the perception of leadership capability. People instinctively assess presence in the first milliseconds of an encounter.

Physical behaviors like standing tall, a steady gaze, graceful movements, warm smiles, and firm handshakes signal presence. A leader's energy impacts outcomes through both obvious and subtle pathways.

Yet many women minimize physicality due to societal messaging. Reconnecting to the body and its wisdom fosters a commanding, authentic presence. Next, you will find six key areas and suggestions to improve your presence.

1. Owning Your Space

Women leaders often diminish their physical presence by occupying less space. Standing or sitting collapsed, crossed ankles, bowed head, and avoiding eye contact all convey a lack of confidence.

Remember these numbers: **30-90-60**. People make their initial assessment of you in thirty seconds on the phone, ninety seconds in person, and then spend the next sixty minutes confirming their decision. Make an effort to improve your first impressions. This will be very valuable when we explore influence.

What to do?

- Keep a straight and tall posture. Please find a full-length mirror and check your posture while standing and walking. Strive to be tall and straight. The straight spine alone gives your body a signal that you are confident. If you have been slumping for years, this will take some practice.
- Arrive at meetings earlier and secure the head seat that faces the door. This is the power position of any room. If the seat is occupied by the meeting leader, take the seat to the right of that chair, as long as the seat doesn't have its back to the door. If the seat to the right is not available, take the seat to the left.
- Make a point to look everyone in the eyes. Every day, as you engage with people, even for a simple hello, hold your gaze at

them for a few seconds. You can nod your head and smile to acknowledge that you see them.
- Practice a firm handshake while looking people in the eyes and sharing a smile. Stop the bouncing handshake. That's when you move your hands up and down.

2. Voice and Speech

How a leader speaks impacts influence as much as what she says. Vocal presence communicates conviction and commands attention.

Deepening vocal tone and volume, speaking from the diaphragm, and articulating well clearly project authority. Plain, concise language prevents dilution of your message.

Changing speech speed, pitch, and rhythm add color and emphasis. Pausing for impact gives words weight. Mastering vocal presence is about harnessing natural gifts, not masculine mimicry.

What to do?

- Practice your speeches multiple times.
- Take three deep breaths before speaking. This brings more oxygen to your brain, helps you calm your nerves, and keeps your thoughts clear.
- Begin your speeches in a positive tone, even if you have to disagree with others. It always works when you can find some positive aspects about what you are about to disagree with.

3. Centering and Grounding

Many mindfulness practices offer quick exercises for people to feel centered and find a sense of well-being. Feeling centered and grounded starts when you wake up in the morning. It takes five to twenty-five minutes to build self-awareness and inner calm. This ancient practice has taught many successful people how to establish poise even amidst turmoil. It works best when you have continuous practice, such as meditation and yoga.

Simple mindfulness practices such as deep breathing are being taught in schools for their physical and mental benefits. Standing like a mountain or envisioning roots growing from your feet down into the earth evokes grounding. It relaxes tension, eases respiration, and clears thoughts, leading to greater focus.

Embodied rituals like walking meditations, toe-to-head body scans, or connecting to the heart center cultivate calm. Grounded, centered leaders exude steadfast, tranquil power.

What to do?

- Listen to one of the two meditations in the book at https://ana-barreto.com/bonus.
- Go for a walk in green spaces for at least forty-five minutes a week.
- End your day with a gratitude practice to set you up for a better tomorrow. That's only a one to three-minute practice you do in bed at the end of the day, where you recognize the wins of the day.

4. Mind-Body Flow

Our thoughts and attitudes directly shape our physical well-being. When the mind takes the body to focus positively, the body reciprocates by uplifting the mind. They share a two-way relationship known as the mind-body connection.

For instance, chronic stress and pessimism weaken the immune system, while mindfulness and laughter fill the body with healing endorphins. Believing we lack energy makes us lethargic while visualizing vibrancy energizes us.

But first, a mindset shift is required; from thinking our bodily state is fixed to recognizing we can intentionally sculpt it with the power of the mind. If the mind doesn't believe this, the body will not cooperate.

The body is both the vehicle for actualizing positive visions, and the map for charting new paths. Master leaders know how to read this map. A new mindset allows for unlocking its incredible power.

Leaders can fake presence temporarily, but true resilience comes from mind-body integration. Inner beliefs shape outer reality, which then affirms inner beliefs.

What to do?

- Pay attention to your mindset's disempowering thoughts. Every time you catch a self-critical thought, stop it and correct it out loud with a positive one.
- Visualize being confident and having successful outcomes. The mind doesn't know what imagination or reality is. It thinks in pictures, so create great success in your mind, because if your mind can see it, you will arrive there.
- Say affirmations out loud, looking in your eyes in the mirror, such as "You are awesome," "You can do anything you put your mind to," and "I have your back." Begin to support yourself every morning as you brush your teeth and hair. This will rewire your brain and improve the way you see yourself.

5. Physical Health

It's not uncommon for women to get up at 7 AM, get the kids to school, fight traffic, grab a cup of coffee on the way to work, and starve their bodies until 1 pm. Unless you are fasting on purpose; this is not very healthy for you.

A healthy, nourished, strong body is the foundation of leadership presence. Self-care regimens boost energy, cognition, and mood— all fuel for performing under pressure.

Good nutrition, hydration, motion, touch, and sleep keep leaders mentally sharp and emotionally steady. Endorphins from exercise enhance executive function and general calm.

What to do?

- Start your day with two glasses of room temperature or lukewarm water. Lukewarm water can help digestion and improve blood circulation, in contrast to cold water. Experts recommend drinking water first thing in the morning, to hydrate the body and brain, optimizing energy and health. Water boosts metabolism, aids digestion, flushes toxins from the kidneys, lubricates joints, oxygenates cells, and boosts brain function. It also prevents headaches, fatigue, cravings, and constipation.
- Eat balanced meals. A balanced diet with nutrients from all the major food groups energizes both body and mind. Consuming a variety of healthy proteins, fats, carbohydrates, fruits, vegetables, and fibers is key for sustainable energy. As a leader, you are aiming for peak performance.
- Regular exercise is vital for Holistic Leaders to maintain the physical stamina, mental focus, and stress resilience needed to perform under pressure. Daily movements have extensive cognitive and emotional benefits. Exercise boosts brain chemicals like serotonin and dopamine to elevate mood and motivation. It also stimulates neurogenesis, the growth of new brain cells. Leaders who work out consistently have sharpened executive function, memory, and willpower. They maintain composure in high-stress situations.

Beyond mental sharpness, exercise improves cardiovascular health, immunity, posture, and longevity. I am sure you have heard all that, but with a full life outside work, who has time to exercise, right? Begin by committing to walk two to three times a week, perhaps during your lunch break or on the weekend. Then add a day after work before you get home. Full disclosure, I don't enjoy going to the gym. I prefer playing volleyball, riding my bike, and flat walks in green spaces. But when I do go, I take an online class, listen to a great podcast, or watch my teachers on YouTube.

6. Authentic Expression

Lena, a manager on the path to promotion, didn't get the job she had been aiming at for a few years. When the new boss came to meet the team, he pretended that he didn't know Lena had applied for his job and didn't get it. Lena knew from her previous boss that the new guy was aware she didn't get the job and was pretending ignorance. From that moment on, she never trusted anything he said.

Holistic Leaders strive to be authentic, to act and express themselves in alignment with inner values, personality, and wisdom. Authenticity builds trust and deepens relationships.

When leaders reveal their true thoughts transparently, with care and tact, people feel seen, and masks fall away. Sharing vulnerability fosters reciprocal openness and stronger connections.

Authentic self-expression also boosts confidence and presence. Leaders who embrace quirks and unique gifts project comfortable assurance. They know themselves profoundly and lead from a place of inner truth.

Additionally, authenticity reduces stress by eliminating the exhausting projection of false personas and the need to keep up with lies. Aligning the outer portrayal and inner world lets leaders operate with ease. Their footprints match their path.

What to do?

- Honor yourself, warts and all. To build your authentic self, start by accepting who you are, even if you don't conform to the mainstream. Admit your mistakes openly and honestly, manage expectations realistically, and be open to receiving feedback.
- Stop lying and tell the truth. Honesty builds authenticity as a Holistic Leader. Speaking truthfully and tactfully is a cornerstone of authentic leadership. It demonstrates respect for others. Even difficult truths, shared compassionately, foster growth by narrowing the gap between reality and perception. Of course, truth must be conveyed with care and consideration for its impact. Ultimately, truthful communication aligns with integrity in expression.
- Take the time to prepare to tell the truth, but don't wait too long. There is such a thing as the right time to talk. Sometimes, people procrastinate because of fear of others' reactions.

7. Somatic Intelligence

Somatic Intelligence is listening to your body's knowing. The practice builds mindfulness of inner physical sensations, which convey valuable intuition. Your moods, needs, and other responses register in the body.

Paying attention to "gut feelings" and subtle energetic shifts cultivates somatic intelligence. Leaders can sense what moves or unsettles them and adjust accordingly. Often, the body will tell these things before the mind has a chance to process them.

Noticing physical reactions grounds decisions in wisdom. Does a bold vision feel energizing, or anxiety-producing? Do new tactics cause unease or inspiration? The body knows.

What to do?

- Trust your gut. Not every gut feeling will drive you to action, but many will. My experience taught me that when I ignore my gut impulses urging me to act, they will keep coming back until I do act on them.
- Pay attention to your personality. MBTI© "**S**ensing" types will struggle to decide based on gut feelings. On the other side, MBTI© "i**N**tuitive" people will believe every hunch is the right decision.
- Listen to the Meditation "Let It Go: Self Acceptance".

The Work of Dr. Joe Dispenza

Neuroscientist and author Dr. Joe Dispenza provides extensive research on shaping reality through the mind-body connection. His books, like *Becoming Supernatural,* outline how mental rehearsal and embodiment can rewire the brain.

Dispenza's research shows that envisioning desired futures and purposefully "feeling" oneself embodying that future—rather than just thinking about it—signals the brain to expect and create a positive outcome.

Dr. Dispenza teaches us that we can use our thoughts and charge them with emotions to get our unconscious self to do, be, or have our desired success. If we can think about it, we can get there.

Holistic Leaders can harness this mind-body connection to build motivation, presence, and transformational leadership capacity. It seems simple, but it works. Imagine yourself poised, standing tall, and energized by the new way you feel. This sense of presence causes subtle physical changes. Feel what you would feel like when you embody your thoughts and emotions to kickstart the manifestation of the person you envision into reality.

The goal is to do this multiple times a day for at least thirty days, and see and feel the difference. Each time, do it for sixty-six seconds. Not sixty or fifty-five. This is the secret and the power of neuroplasticity. Sixty-six seconds is enough time to build momentum in your brain and create changes. You are firing new neurons and sequencing them to pay attention to what you want instead of leaving your default program in charge.

CHAPTER EIGHT

THE MIND: EMOTIONAL INTELLIGENCE

*"I don't need the armor anymore. I can walk on stage
in jeans and a T-shirt, and I'm strong enough."*
— Lady Gaga

Sarah led a fast-paced marketing team for a major clothing retailer. She had an excellent grasp of marketing strategy and drove impressive results month after month. However, her department had high turnover and constant employee issues.

Employees felt burnt out by intense workloads and Sarah's blunt, critical leadership style. Her boss had been warned about Sarah's shortcomings and chose not to address them fully. Sarah was a dedicated manager, worked late nights and weekends, and delivered great results. Many of her results were achieved through heavy pressure on her team. She constantly emailed them early in the morning or late at night, expecting answers. Her focus was firmly on outcomes, without empathy for the staff's needs. Sarah believed that coddling people was unproductive.

One incident caused two key members of her team to resign and leave the company without notice. Beth, an account manager on the team, lost her mother and had to fly home to arrange the funeral. She was given five days of bereavement. When Beth returned to work, everyone could see that she was still mourning the loss of her mother. By noon, Beth was feeling drained. She went to Sarah and told her she had to leave because she was unable to focus on work and needed more time.

"You have been out for five days, and you are behind," Sarah replied, but eventually, Sarah allowed her to leave.

Beth went back to her office, told other colleagues what had happened, packed her things, and left the job for good. Two weeks later, another member of Sarah's team also left. Tom, another account manager on her team, couldn't attend a meeting because his daughter got sick at school, and he had to pick her up.

"Can her mother pick her up? Sarah asked.

"My wife is out of town," Tom replied.

"Will you come back?" Sarah pestered.

"My wife is out of town, Sarah." Tom didn't come back, and quit the job with an email.

We don't need to hire a consultant to assess that Sarah had strong technical skills and almost non-existent emotional intelligence, which undermined her team's loyalty and performance.

Many people may read this story and ask why Sarah wasn't fired.

Although this is a combination of two real-life stories, it illustrates the importance of Emotional Intelligence (EQ) in leadership. When you comb through your past, you may find two or three people with traits similar to Sarah's who were not fired. Her behavior is often discounted when men display it, not as much for women. Many organizations are guilty of ignoring the lack of emotional intelligence in leaders in lieu of great results, at the cost of their people.

A recent case shared with me by Melissa, an Accounts Receivable Manager in an oil company, upset me to my core. Melissa received a disrespectful and offensive email from a director from a different department, slamming her work. She complained about the inappropriate behavior to her boss, who is friends with the director, and he played it off. She was outraged that her boss wouldn't address the issue.

The director was rude and disrespectful to everyone. He would yell at the staff, throw things on the floor and wall, and slam doors. Melissa went to Human Resources and made a formal complaint. Later that day, she received a text from the director apologizing for his behavior and sharing that he was going through a divorce. Melissa didn't know how he got her number, but she didn't respond. Four days later, she sent an email to HR asking for a resolution since no one had contacted her, and HR scheduled a meeting with Melissa, her boss, and the director.

At the meeting, it was agreed that the director, who was not part of Melissa's department, would not interfere in her work and would keep the communication professional and respectful.

Melissa shared with me that she was not satisfied with the resolution. She wanted him to be coached about his behavior. Since that meeting, the director has copied HR and her boss on every email he sent her, even unimportant ones. Melissa asked the HR Manager why the director had to copy her in every email, and she didn't know. Three weeks later, Melissa was called to HR and felt ambushed by the director and her boss. In that meeting, the director complained that a letter Melissa sent to a customer was inappropriate. That letter was the same letter she had been sending to all customers for the past two years. She excused herself from the meeting and left. Her coworkers had advised her not to complain about the director because he had been in the company for over fifteen years, and he could get her fired. Melissa was clearly being retaliated against by the director, with the support of her boss.

This kind of thing is common, but we often don't hear about it because the women resign before they get retaliated against. Unfortunately, when women resign, they incentivize the harassment happening in male-dominated companies.

The Case for Emotional Intelligence

When I was first assessed for Emotional intelligence in 1999, I scored very low, and I was not alone. Over the years, I found that women generally lack or have low levels of Emotional Intelligence. I didn't assess them, but their behavior measured it for me. The ones who had a fair level of EQ were better able to advance their careers.

The question we need to ask is, if women are naturally caring, empathetic, and nurturing, how could they lack high levels of emotional Intelligence?

Emotional intelligence, defined as perceiving, understanding, and regulating emotions in self and others, correlates strongly with leadership success. This chapter explores the key reasons for the EQ shortage in women and practices for developing emotional intelligence to create empathetic, resonant leadership.

IQ and technical skills alone do not guarantee effective leadership. Emotional intelligence distinguishes the great leaders from the average. And who wants to be average?

Studies by the Hay Group found that professionals with greater emotional intelligence get promoted more often. They create tightly bonded teams and retain more talent. However, very few organizations invest resources early enough in the career path to support their talent pool. When they do, men are more likely to receive those resources than women.

Harvard Business Review analyzed data from 188 companies and found that emotional intelligence differentiates outstanding from average performers far more than intellect or expertise alone. On measures like initiative, adaptability, influence, and teamwork, emotional intelligence proved a much stronger indicator of leadership excellence.

Emotional intelligence starts with a deep understanding of one's own emotions, motivations, strengths, and growth areas. Self-awareness unlocks authentic expression and wise choices.

Assessing personality, values, stress responses, relationship patterns, and inner narratives provides some insights critical for increasing your emotional intelligence. What emotional states arise regularly? How do they manifest physically?

Noticing emotional patterns without judgment allows the reprogramming of unhelpful reactions. Experts suggest keeping a daily mood log to increase self-understanding. But who has time to log their emotions daily? Also, the biggest challenge is consistency. Often, busy schedules and forgetfulness will interfere with identifying a pattern. Plus, people have reported struggling to identify and articulate emotions.

Ask a woman to name five incidents in which they were mistreated, ignored, put down, or scared, and they will recall ten. Ask a man, and he may recall one or two, but are likely to play them down.

Women have elephant memories. They recall how something felt when it happened, and they don't want to repeat it.

Women improve their emotional intelligence when they identify emotional blind spots caused by bias or past pain. Unexamined hurt produces overreactions and conflicts. Healing those wounds prevents projection onto others.

While discussing emotional wounds may seem out of place in a business context, failing to address this aspect would be a disservice to the development of women's emotional intelligence. Emotional baggage and unresolved trauma can significantly impair one's ability to regulate emotions, empathize with others, and make sound decisions. By creating a safe space for women to confront and heal from past emotional injuries, we equip them with the self-awareness and resilience necessary to overcome the typical pitfalls that hinder emotional intelligence. Only by fearlessly exploring the depths of their emotional landscapes can women truly understand their motivations, harness their strengths, and identify areas for growth. This holistic approach to emotional development is crucial for cultivating the high emotional quotient that drives success in both personal and professional realms.

Typical Flaws of Emotional Intelligence in Women

Having addressed the importance of healing emotional wounds as a foundation for cultivating emotional intelligence, we must now turn our attention to some of the common pitfalls that can undermine women's EQ development. Despite the strides made in recognizing the value of emotional intelligence in the workplace, many women still struggle with blind spots that limit their ability to fully harness this critical skill set.

Through my work with female professionals across several industries, I have identified two pervasive EQ issues that manifest in women: a tendency toward catastrophizing or envisioning worst-case scenarios, and avoiding conflict. By shining a light on these typical flaws, we can better understand the challenges women face and develop targeted strategies to overcome them, ultimately empowering women to unlock their full emotional intelligence potential.

Worst Case Scenario

Christine was being developed for a director role. Her boss arranged for her to spend time with a male director so she could broaden her perspective and learn from other successful leaders. Christine emailed the director and didn't hear back for a few days. She called her boss to complain that the director hadn't reached out to her and said that she assumed he didn't want to help her out. Her boss told her that email was not the proper way to reach out to the director and that a phone call would work best. Plus, she shouldn't assume the worst from people. The email might have gotten lost, or perhaps he was on vacation or just very busy. The next day, the director reached out to Christine and arranged a time for them to get together.

Christine's emotional intelligence, in this case, is very similar to many female leaders. Although she didn't know that director, she assumed the worst-case scenario. This type of emotional reaction has nothing to do with the work, but with Christine's previous experiences being turned down. Her mind goes from zero to 1,000 in seconds, without any time to process the situation. I've witnessed similar emotional reactions to being taken advantage of, being compared to their parents, being challenged, witnessing unfairness or bragging, and so on.

Avoiding Conflict

The second Emotional Intelligence issue I found in women is their tendency to avoid conflict. Many women endure dissatisfaction or unmet needs quietly for too long, not wanting to complain or cause trouble. But feelings buried alive never die. Eventually, they erupt like volcanos in uncontrolled explosions, taking everyone by surprise.

I see this often with female leaders, tolerating poor treatment, lack of support, or unfair conditions without objection ... until one day, they quit or have emotional meltdowns seemingly out of the blue. Yet, clues of mounting distress were likely ignored.

This conflict avoidance pattern also sabotages relationships. How many times have you snapped at a loved one over a minor offense that actually masked deeper grievances left unspoken? Women must become comfortable addressing frustrations early before they become avalanches. If everything is "fine," yet you secretly churn, it is not fine. Small conversations could solve problems if we spoke up instead of staying silent until frustration boils over unexpectedly. This is leading with emotional courage.

The underlying issue is that women feel hesitant to be viewed as complainers or troublemakers for expressing legitimate dissatisfaction. Suppressing your authentic feelings helps no one in the end. Voice issues while they are still small. You show leadership by upholding your well-being over keeping the peace.

How Can a Holistic Leader Develop Stronger Emotional Intelligence?

Developing emotional intelligence takes continual practice. It's not something that you read in a book, memorize, and immediately use successfully. Research recommends combining self-knowledge, empathy, and mindfulness to build higher levels of Emotional Intelligence over time. Here are seven ways for you to improve your Emotional Intelligence:

1. Engaging in Self-Reflection

When we ask people to self-reflect, often they can't see who they are when they are angry, frustrated, or just feeling down. Not many people have the skills or resources to get the feedback they need to make progress. Here are three suggestions:

-   **Find your personal triggers and solve them**. What and who pushes your buttons? What emotions do you express when you are dissatisfied? What are the recurring patterns of behavior that leave you depleted? I used to feel livid when I saw someone taking advantage of others or the system, even if it didn't involve me. I realized that I was triggered by times in my childhood when I felt that my older sister had taken advantage of me.
-   **Identify areas for growth.** Through journaling, meditation, and coaching, you can spot opportunities. I believe that meditation is the best and fastest way to improve your Emotional Intelligence. There are many types of meditation, but a guided one to rewire your emotions works much faster than contemplative meditation. My EQ improved because of my meditation practices. Visit Ana-Barreto.com/Bonus to begin the Let Go Meditation series to improve your emotional intelligence.

- **Develop self-awareness.** Learn how emotions impact thoughts, words, and actions. Once you identify your triggers and work to rewire your emotions via meditation, you will be able to observe the emotions generated from a thought you keep rethinking. It's amazing when you notice that your boss reminds you of your parents, or you don't like the guy in accounting because he talks like your ex-husband. Before you react as you would with your parents or ex-partner, you can stop and watch the thoughts go by without an emotional reaction from you.

2. Build Empathy

Empathy, the ability to sense and relate to others' emotions, builds rapport and inclusive leadership. Truly listening without judgment demonstrates care. Noticing nonverbal cues like tone and body language reveals unspoken feelings. Simply asking, "How are you feeling?" and meaning it, builds trust.

People usually ask how you are feeling and don't pay attention to the response. We expect them to say: "I'm fine," and move on, even if their full expression doesn't match the response.

Holistic Leaders can make an impact on others in five minutes or less. Your energy, mindset, and mood can impact the people around you. If you are feeling great, you uplift others; if you are feeling crappy, you deplete others. The energy that wins is the energy being expressed the loudest.

I am not suggesting that you walk in at work bellowing with fake excitement, but that you bring your very best to work and ensure your own energy contributes, instead of diminishing the level people are at. A leader looking to grow their EQ must take care of their emotions first—it's that simple.

To bring your best self to work, you must start the night before. Here are three easy actions that can help you in the morning:

- **Instead of binge-watching a Netflix series until the wee hours of the morning, plan to go to bed and get seven or eight hours of sleep**. The bogus information that you can operate on four to six hours of sleep will not help you, even if you believe it. Good sleep alone will improve your mood, health, and cognitive functions. You will have better memory, creativity, problem-solving, judgment, and emotional processing.
- **Leave most of the day behind**. Most people tend to take the struggles of the day to bed, not the good omens. A good practice to sleep well was suggested by Norman Vincent Peale in his book *The Power of Positive Thinking*, published in 1952. His sleeping practice is still valid today. I use this technique when I struggle to shake off a bad day. As you lay in bed, close your eyes and imagine emptying your pocket or purse of the problems of the day, and throwing them into the garbage. It helps when you imagine walking outside the house and dropping things into the larger can. Again, this is simple, but it works. You will find this guided practice at Ana-Barreto.com/Bonus.
- **Keep the good stuff**. Now that you have discarded the bad juju of the day, it's time to sleep with gratitude. Find at least three people, things, or situations from your day that you can be grateful for. Some days, you will need to find a good cup of coffee or the fact that your car didn't break down. This end-of-the-day gratitude practice helps you reset your thoughts and emotions. You can't be upset and grateful at the same time. Plus, gratitude is not like a cheap lover—when you wake up it will still be there.

3. Start Your Day Right

Great teachers have suggested a number of ways to get your day right, from positive rituals such as getting up at 5 AM to exercise, learning, reading, journaling, and meditating. Any positive ritual will improve your mind, body, and spirit. I suggest that you pick three.

- **Meditate**. The most powerful ritual for me is meditating. I set up my alarm for forty-five minutes before I need to get up to give me the time to set up my day for success. Meditation connects me with my higher power, and I often receive guidance in my life. It leads me to know what decisions I need to make that will serve me and the people around me.
- **Make your bed**. Making your bed builds a mindset of organization and focus, self-care, and discipline. It gives your psyche a sense of accomplishment, and it's a treat when you return to the ordered bedroom at the end of the day.
- **Drink two glasses of water.** Two glasses of water jump-starts a daily practice of self-care and hydrates your body. It will help your brain with increased blood flow and oxygen.

4. Cultivating Relationships

Leaders with empathy seek diverse perspectives. They cultivate relationships and tailor communications personally to each member of their team. Making people feel seen, valued, and understood unlocks discretionary effort. Empathy requires leading with the head and heart in tandem.

Building your empathy level could be a challenge if you are a MBTI© high "T" (Thinker) starting your career. Also, if you were raised by people who valued logic, then emotions didn't run free in your household, finding room for empathy will take more emotional effort. In addition, Thinkers tend to mentor other Thinkers, and if they don't have the level of EQ needed, they will propagate behaviors that will deplete rather than create Holistic Leadership traits. To start:

- **Listen deeply to colleagues and team members without judgment.** Take what they say at face value. Try to stop rehearsing how you are going to respond, and shower them with your attention.
- **Ask yourself what emotion is dominating what you hear, without judgment.**
- **Observe body language and tone for unspoken cues into emotions.** If you don't deal well with people expressing high emotions, before you run away, take this opportunity to begin to learn about them.
- **Avoid projecting your own assumptions onto people's states.** People make mistakes, and they are entitled to make them, regardless of their views. You don't know what they have been carrying or going through. Use words such as "I understand," "I am sorry you are going through this," "I am sorry you feel that way," "How can I help?" or, "Could we connect later today so I can process what you shared with me?"

5. Mindfulness practices

Build the ability to stay present and grounded when stressed, through breathing exercises, visualization, and meditation. This doesn't happen automatically. You must build a meditation or visualization practice daily to access the benefits of staying present and grounded when matters arise.

Try to:

- **Insert pauses during conversations to evaluate how to respond consciously.**
- **Slow your breathing and speech when you feel stressful situations coming on.**

6. Self-Regulation

Once aware of others' emotional landscape, leaders can consciously regulate reactions and behaviors. Instead of lashing out, they respond skillfully. Pausing before acting controls knee-jerk reactions. Reframing anxious thoughts into positive intentions reduces reactivity.

Holistic Leaders tend to take the higher road. They do get mad, but they can calm down quickly and react with the appropriate force and timing.

Setting boundaries around work moderate frustration. Channeling anger into vigorous exercise or humor diffuses tension. Also, self-regulation builds resilience. Leaders who stay cool under pressure and think avoid blunders and model graceful behavior.

During a talent review meeting, Bob, a new manager, removed a high-performing female leader from the pull, reasoning that she cried too much, and replaced her with a male manager. The other leaders didn't know her well, and no one made a fuss, confirming that crying was not acceptable in that workplace. I was the only woman in the room.

Forty-five percent of female workers cry on the job. Although these women don't want to cry in the workplace, it happens. At a team member level, it's not a big deal. But, as women move up the ladder, it has a bigger impact, as more men are in charge of their ascendance. Harvard Business Review reported that research on over 2,000 senior leaders found that 44 percent of leaders believe that crying is okay from time to time. Another 30 percent believe it has no negative impact on how you are perceived at work. Is it true? Or are leaders not aware of their unconscious bias toward women crying at work?

Many women cry when they feel frustrated, anxious, burned out, or deeply passionate and invested in their work. Women have reported crying when being bullied, overworked, disrespected, and put down in front of their peers. When men experience these scenarios, they get mad, yell, punch a wall, or attack. I would think that a woman crying is more favorable than punching a wall.

Women also cry when they feel bad for other people. This is a sign of high emotional intelligence. Only people with low EQ would discount crying at work.

The last time a female leader cried in front of me, I cried with her. She told me that her boss's boss put her down in front of her team, and the boss didn't react.

Crying is a sign of vulnerability. It builds trust and connection. These traits are important for teamwork and loyalty. Senior Leaders should be required by their conscience to learn why women are crying at work and make space for them to be themselves. Is it because of work stress? Then fix it. Is it because of their personal life? Send them on vacation. People spend more waking hours at work than with their loved ones. The work time should be meaningful and enjoyable, or we ought to just relinquish our titles as leaders and do something else.

7. Motivation

Emotionally intelligent leaders harness positive emotions like passion, curiosity, and purpose to drive motivation. Energy flows when emotions align with the mission.

Motivation is undervalued in most organizations today. Once, I heard a high-ranking leader say, "Would you deliver it if your job depended on it?" Threatening people with their jobs is not motivation; it's bullying.

Holistic Leaders motivate others by clarifying the core values and aligning the work to deeply held convictions that fuel engagement. These leaders inspire others with vision and enthusiasm, even when things look gloomy. They celebrate progress and wins to sustain momentum.

Everyone wants to win. Motivation just gives you a really good shot at success.

EQ Is the Way

Holistic Leaders help grow Emotional Intelligence in their team by role modeling vulnerability, creativity, and light-heartedness, fostering intrinsically motivated teams. Passion is contagious when emotions move together, not just minds.

Authentic expression of emotions like joy, grief, fear, and affection builds bonds. Appropriate vulnerability connects teams to purpose. It doesn't mean that you can dump your baggage on the team. The MBTI© Extroverts must be mindful of their emotions. Extroverts tend to contaminate their team with their bad moods and elevate them when they are happy. Leaders should express truths with care and avoid dumping emotions indiscriminately. Yet, suppressing feelings entirely can block connections.

Be open to celebrating, mourning, hoping, dreaming, and holding space for people to share where they are—these shared emotions transform teams. Also, you are helping individuals grow their emotional intelligence, which also benefits everyone outside the office.

I hope I have shared compelling reasons for the increased value you will gain by improving your emotional intelligence. Holistic Leaders must invest their time in building high levels of Emotional Intelligence. This is an opportunity to close the book and select one of the suggestions above to practice. This is an investment in yourself and a commitment to honor your spirit of service to others. Take a break now, and we will continue in Chapter Nine.

CHAPTER NINE

THE SPIRIT: PURPOSE AND MEANING

"Don't ever underestimate the
power of your own instinct."
— Barbara Corcoran

P urpose and meaning are cornerstones of Holistic Leadership. When work connects to principles bigger than oneself, passion ignites. This chapter explores leading from the realm of spirit— ethics, vision, and service.

Defining Spirit

Spirit represents the aspects of humanity that transcend ego and physicality. It encompasses consciousness, intuition, and the universal human search for meaning. Though often associated with religion, the spirit also relates to secular purpose and ethics. Spirit is the realm of imagination, creativity, and legacy.

Leaders who operate from spirit connect work to values and vision bigger than themselves or corporate gain. They tap into collective wisdom in service of society.

Servant Leadership

Robert Greenleaf first coined the term Servant Leadership in his 1970 essay, The Servant as Leader. He criticized leadership paradigms fixated on domination and profiteering. Servant leadership focuses on developing the potential in people to serve their communities better. Rather than self-glorification, Servant Leaders derive meaning from empowering others.

The Holistic Leader is a Servant Leader. While traditional leadership paradigms focus on the accumulation and exercise of power by individuals, servant leadership prioritizes meeting the needs of others.

Some key behaviors displayed by servant leaders are:

- Listening attentively to understand what employees, colleagues, and communities require to thrive.
- Encouraging constant learning and growth in themselves and others through mentorship.
- Rethinking incentive structures to emphasize intrinsic motivation and team success over self-interest.
- Leading with humility and ethics as their highest priorities.
- Building a sense of stewardship and shared ownership throughout organizations.

Servant leaders derive satisfaction from uplifting other people, not accruing status or wealth, although financial gain and career progression often follow them. They measure results through the successful empowerment and development of those they serve.

Servant leadership integrates emotional intelligence, ethics, empowerment, and purpose. It resonates in times of inequality and social or environmental crises.

Greenleaf writes that true leadership emerges from the desire to help others fulfill their own potential. When leaders shift focus from self-glory to collective growth, they unlock lasting greatness.

Spiritual Leadership

Whereas servant leadership emphasizes other-centered service, Spiritual Leadership integrates inner development with a higher purpose. Leaders must consider the values of the workforce, which are changing rapidly.

A 2021 study from Horizons Workforce Consulting found that 64 percent of Generation Z graduates see having a job reflecting their values as very important or absolutely essential. Another survey from 2020 conducted by Harris Poll, commissioned by ZipRecruiter, showed that 86 percent of college graduates considered meaning and purpose to be either very important or *extremely* important in evaluating job offers.

There are people still looking just to make lots of money overnight, but many have concluded that the jobs that are available don't bring satisfaction. When you talk to managers across industries, you find that there has been an increase in workers calling in sick, experiencing anxiety, being unable to deal with the type of work they signed up for, and quitting without notice. The difference between Gen Z and previous generations is that Z just quits and walks out. The previous ones quit more silently, simply doing the minimum possible to collect a paycheck.

Spiritual Leaders must embark on journeys of self-discovery and actualization, because their workforce expects them to have a vision that is aligned with their purpose. But the quest for wholeness gets directed outward through vision and mentorship.

Leaders, at this time, must have three main qualities in addition to everything else. They must:

1. Love People
2. Love, Love People
3. Love, Love, Love People

According to a 2021 survey by Tallo, over half of the college graduating seniors said they turned down a job offer because it did not align with their values or purpose. Although this generation has been more engaged in social issues since the Boomers of the 70s, many of them still lack maturation. Their values include a high-paying salary, typically above the pay grade for the position, and benefits such as long vacations and other perks. Previous generations would be advised to take what they could get and run. For Baby Boomers and Generation X employees, the job market was often more competitive, and job security was prized above all else. There was a pervasive mindset that one should be grateful for any opportunity presented, even if the compensation package fell short of expectations. Employers held significant leverage, and employees were frequently advised to accept offers without excessive bargaining, or else risk losing the position altogether.

Mary, a senior manager looking for candidates in the Boston area, made an offer to a young man, just out of college with no management experience, to enroll in the Management Training Program. He had a great personality and interviewed well. The young man turned down the offer. He wanted $50,000 more than the job paid, which was what she made without bonuses and other incentives based on performance. Mary, recognizing the young man was naïve and didn't know how the industry worked, took the time to explain the business. Mary was willing to give him another $8,000 and match his salary to someone who had already been in the position for over a year. She liked ambitious young people. The candidate felt insulted by the additional offer and walked out of the meeting.

Today's leaders are required to be more than managers if they are to retain staff and develop the new leaders of tomorrow. They are to be trusted insightful mentors with patience and influence.

The dilemma many leaders have is how to become the bosses the younger generation would gladly work for. Leaders must be aligned with their purpose and have meaning in their work. If leaders are misaligned, why would anyone follow them? If a boss works on a job they hate with people they dislike, they will only be able to fake satisfaction only for a little while.

Properly aligned people are not happy all the time, but when they are dissatisfied, they don't stay that way for long. Self-alignment happens in mindfulness practices. Activities such as self-care, meditation, tai-chi, chi gong, yoga, journaling, and nature walks cultivate spiritual leadership. Leaders must be congruent first before they can lead others with a clean conscience.

Contemplating questions like "Why am I here?" "How do I contribute to my team?" "Am I growing?" "Do I enjoy my experiences?" and "What legacy will I leave?" provide direction.

Here are some examples of companies that cultivate spiritual practices at work, responding to the needs of their employees:

- **Google** - Provides on-site yoga and meditation classes, along with apps like Search Inside Yourself, focused on mindfulness.
- **Nike** - Offers yoga, meditation spaces, and professional coaching on mindfulness practices.
- **Target** - Integrates meditation breaks and provides mindfulness rooms at headquarters. It also offers sleep and resilience courses.
- **General Mills** - Incorporates on-site mindfulness programs like mindful eating, yoga, and meditation.
- **Apple** - Provides meditation sessions and a twelve-week mindfulness training program developed by a former Buddhist monk.
- **LinkedIn** - Offers weekly yoga and mindfulness workshops. It also has meditation pods in offices.

- **Ford** - Launched mindfulness programs focused on stress reduction through meditation and mind-body practices.
- **Blackrock** - Provides mindfulness coaching, yoga, meditation, and resilience programs.

These and many other leading companies are investing in mindfulness and well-being programs for employees. They are connecting work to personal growth and self-improvement, leading individuals to find purpose and meaning. Leadership flows from inner wisdom.

Stewardship

We can't speak about Leadership without touching on Stewardship. This means considering long-term impacts on society and the environment, not just immediate profits. It honors the interdependent nature of life. Steward Leaders make sustainable choices to protect communities both now and in the future. They shepherd resources mindfully, guided by ethics.

Given increasing dependence on ecological systems and rapid technological change, stewardship is imperative. Leaders shape destiny based on whether short-term gain gets prioritized over collective legacy.

The biggest concern that can be addressed at any level of the organization is managing waste and recycling. Most leaders have low influence on the grand-scale decisions the company makes. However, you can influence your local environment. Make Stewardship part of your actions, and people will notice it.

Shared Vision

Holistic leaders articulate compelling visions and enlist others to turn them into realities. Visions spawn creativity, hope, and momentum. While ego-driven leaders impose rigid visions, spirit-guided leaders co-create aspirational futures collectively. They know a vision only resonates when it aligns with shared values and purposes.

Martin Luther King Jr.'s vision for racial equity continues to catalyze change because it taps into the spirit of justice innately present in all. His words pointed toward truth. Leading from universal human values—compassion, dignity, justice, beauty—ensures integrity, even when circumstances challenge ethics.

A Holistic Leader's vision for Leadership embodies a profound understanding that all aspects of life are interconnected. They lead with wisdom, compassion, and a commitment to uplifting the entire ecosystem they operate within. Rather than pursuing narrow business objectives, Holistic Leaders take a panoramic view, considering the impact of their decisions on their people, their community, and the planet itself. This projected vision will lead to economic prosperity.

Our MBTI© Extroverts are likely to spread the vision to all. MBTI© Introverts may delay it until they are more than ready. If you are an MBTI© Introvert, be mindful that you may cancel or postpone meetings, deeming them unnecessary. Also, our MBTI© INtuitives may not convey all the details of a vision, which is needed for a buy-in, because those visions are vibrant in their own heads.

Humanity longs to be part of something bigger than itself. Though Holistic Leadership requires strength and skill, at its core, it is an act of spirit—hope projected into the world. May we all lead in a way that is aligned with our highest callings.

With this, we conclude the key points of Holistic Leadership. In the next chapter, we will cover the foundation of Leadership itself, which must be present before you can become a Holistic Leader.

CHAPTER TEN

STRESS MANAGEMENT AND SELF-CARE

"Confidence comes not from always being right but from not fearing to be wrong."
— Rosalynn Carter

Gloria was a high-performing manager when she was promoted to senior management. She inherited a team that wasn't performing very well. Her predecessor had resigned instead of being fired. Gloria's new boss was demanding. She had to learn new responsibilities, connect with her team, and assess their performance under high pressure from her boss, who expected she would turn things around quickly.

In her personal life, her husband had quit his job without having another position lined up and was left unemployed for over six months. He got job offers but didn't take them. He accepted a position but resigned by the end of the second week. He was starting another job just as she shared her frustration with me. Gloria's younger daughter had moved back into the house, and she suspected her husband showed signs of depression. In addition, her parents were getting older and needed her support going to doctor's appointments. Gloria's only brother lived out of state. Money was tight, even though she had gotten a promotion.

Gloria's new job required her to travel every other week. Because of her personal commitments, she drove three to four hours to visit her teams and drove back home the same day instead of staying for a night or two. Her days were long.

She became short-tempered with her team, and her family life suffered. Gloria also got COVID-19 twice in four months. Her symptoms lingered, and she was unable to keep up with the demands of her new position and family life. Her team's results continued to decline and many wondered if she should have gotten the job.

The daily pressures of leadership can accumulate and lead to chronic stress, exhaustion, and burnout, if not managed proactively. This chapter explores techniques women leaders can use to reduce the negative effects of stress and care for themselves holistically before their bodies, minds, and spirits take them hostage with disease.

The Cost of Stress

Leadership roles come with heavy demands and high-stakes decisions that often create excessive stress. Unmanaged, this stress extorts physical and emotional tolls.

As neuroscientist Dr. Joe Dispenza explains, "People under stress are always trying to control or predict an outcome. It's like stepping on the brake and the gas peddles at the same time." This constant state of fight or flight piles strain upon the strain.

Stress contributes to issues like hypertension, obesity, diabetes, insomnia, anxiety, depression, and addiction. It can impair cognition, memory, immunity, and performance. Studies show that women leaders report 25-30 percent higher perceived stress than male peers in similar positions. The most concerning statistic is that stress also discourages women from pursuing higher roles.

Causes of Stress

People are terribly afraid of stress, but stress is not the enemy; people's perception is. Stress is the body's natural mechanism to alert us to danger. It's designed to help us survive. Physiologically, when stressed, the body releases the hormones cortisol and adrenaline, which are responsible for regulating several body systems, including cardiovascular and circulatory, and give you enough power to ensure your survival. It will do everything it can to help you conserve energy, and safeguard you so you can defeat whatever threat has come your way.

The stress mechanism was meant to help you outrun a tiger, fight a bear, or defend your offspring from predators by narrowing your focus and redirecting the energy normally allocated to other bodily functions such as digestion and hunger. This stress mechanism was designed to last a short time. But these days, people experience stress 24/7. It's destroying the bodies, minds, and hearts of leaders.

According to the Holmes and Rahe Stress Scale Research, the top stressors in America are the death of a spouse or child, divorce, marital separation, imprisonment, or death of a close family member, in this order. However, when we look at the workplace, we find that traffic, job security, bullying, harassment, poor communication, relationship conflicts, changes, lack of development opportunities, and work environment are the main causes of persistent stress. People just can't shake them off.

In women, common causes of stress for leaders include:

- **Work overload** - Too many competing priorities and unattainable deadlines
- **Role conflicts** - Tension between work and personal life
- **Harassment** - Sexist remarks, exclusion, and microaggressions
- **Self-criticism** - Inner voices of perfectionism and self-doubt
- **Lack of support** - Isolation and absence of mentors/sponsors
- **Discrimination** - Minimized contributions, biased evaluations, and less favorable treatment

- **Workplace politics** - Gossip, backstabbing, and power plays
- **Unclear expectations** - Ambiguity and micromanagement
- **Pressure to conform** - Suppressing authenticity to fit in

Take a deep breath and read the list above again. This time, add at the end of each sentence, *"... and I will overcome them."*

Example: "Work overload - Too many competing priorities and unattainable deadlines, *and I will overcome them.*"

It's not easy to convince women that their stress is not as big as they perceive it. However, I ask you to consider the possibility that the stress you experience can be managed.

So, how do you deal with the top stressors' women experience?

Please take this to heart.

"If you are too stressed, you don't have access to the solution, even if the solution stepped on your toes."

You must de-stress to solve the problem. The exercise "I will overcome" is the first layer to de-stressing, even if you don't believe it yet. If you practice this exercise and believe, you will overcome it.

Also, if you identify with any of the nine top stressors for women, please adopt one or two of the suggestions below. They will remedy the top causes of stress, help you interpret them, and set you up as a leader to stand in your shoes and own your brilliance. However, the quickest short-term remedy is to take a day or two off and do something you enjoy to get you out of the hole.

Physical Stress Relief

This section will address Work Overload, Role Conflicts, and Unclear Expectations.

The body carries stress physically, through tense muscles, a clenched jaw, a knotted stomach, a racing heart, and shallow breathing. Releasing these somatic tensions brings relief. Here is how:

- **Exercise**: Aerobic movement and strength training dissipates cortisol and boosts mood-lifting endorphins. Take short walks during lunch break or after work.
- **Stretching**: Yoga, Tai chi, Chi gong, and full body stretches relax muscles and increase flexibility needed to adapt to challenges. Learn some yoga poses and tai chi movements and do them in the shower, or in your office during the day.
- **Massage**: Professional massages, Reflexology, or shoulder rubs by your partner loosen muscles and enhance body awareness. Schedule a massage or reflexology after work or on your day off. Once you schedule it, it will be hard for you to bail out on yourself.
- **Breathwork**: Deep belly breathing, breath counting, and pranayama breathing exercises activate the parasympathetic nervous system to counter stress. Access my 33-Breaths Meditation at Ana-Barreto.com/Bonus.
- **Nature immersion**: Spending time outdoors, especially around water, trees, and sunlight, restores calm.
- **Delegate**: Women have a hard time asking others to get things done for them. They are afraid of rejection and often don't trust others, but that's because they don't trust themselves. It's time to rephrase your interpretation of rejection. Rejection is your false projection. When others say no, it's not about the real you. Be willing to ask again and again so your best self can shine.
- **Learn to say No**: "No, I have a lot on my plate right now." This is not about the person but the action. It only takes practice speaking out loud in the bathroom looking in the mirror.

Another practice Holistic Leaders do to increase their confidence is resetting the vagus nerve and, therefore, the heart rate and breathing.

The vagus nerve, also known as the vagal nerve, is the main nerve of your parasympathetic nervous system, and one of twelve cranial nerves in the body. It's responsible for various physical functions, including digestion, heart rate, breathing, cardiovascular activity, and reflex actions such as coughing, sneezing, swallowing, and vomiting. People who are stressed will have shallow breathing and thus deprive the brain of oxygen. Basically, you lose access to everything you know, just like our example at the beginning of this chapter.

Your parasympathetic nervous system is a network of nerves that relaxes your body after periods of stress. It also helps with digestion during times when you feel safe and relaxed. When the parasympathetic nervous system is stimulated, it slows our heart rate, lowers blood pressure, and promotes digestion. Our body enters a state of relaxation and begins recovery.

First, sit comfortably in a chair with your back straight and your feet flat on the ground. Gently turn your head all the way to the right. Notice any discomfort. Then, gently turn your head all the way to the left. Notice any discomfort. Now, hold your hands together, crossing your fingers as shown in the picture below:

Bring your crossed hands behind your head. Your elbows will be facing out.

Keep your face forward and move your eyes (not your head) all the way to the right. Stay there until you have an involuntary yawn or deep sigh. It may take up to three minutes.

Then, you will keep your face forward and move your eyes (not your head) all the way to the left. Stay there until you have an involuntary yawn or deep sigh. It may take up to three minutes. The second usually happens very quickly.

Now, gently turn your head all the way to the right. You will notice that your neck now turns further than it did before. Go ahead and gently turn your head all the way to the left. Again, your head will turn further than it did before.

This exercise can be done to calm yourself and build confidence before you have something important to do. You can use it to get rid of headaches, migraines, and muscle tension.

The beauty lies in exercising innate self-soothing abilities. Some people experience benefits in just minutes. The vagus nerve stimulation technique offers simple yet powerful stress relief that women can access anytime, anywhere.

Time Is the Frenemy

Most women look at me with an air of disbelief when I suggest the helping list above. "Who has the time?" they think. Then, we may conclude that time is an impediment to releasing or reducing stress.

Is "time" then the stressor? Too much to do and so little time? Is "time" harassing, asking for impossible deadlines, causing you to self-doubt, imposing on your family life, or minimizing your contributions? Time is not a stressor, but how you view your time may be stressful to you.

There is a model for reducing stress, called Timefulness; it replaces "Time Management," because managing time doesn't really work. Timefulness comes from the principle that:

"*You have as much time as you think you do.*"

Timefulness is so powerful that merely speaking the phrase, "I have as much time as I think I do" when you feel you are behind on your obligations reduces your stress level immediately.

This intriguing mantra leverages what neuroscience reveals about the malleable nature of time perception. Our brains actually construct an experience of time passing based on emotions, memories, focus, and other factors. It means that we each live in our own "mind time" bubble.

When feeling stressed, time seems to speed up uncontrollably as the mind fixates on perceived scarcity. Thoughts race, worrying over all one must cram into precious few minutes and seconds. The pressure mounts, fight-or-flight kicks in, and we lose awareness of time itself speeding by.

However, in pleasant or novel experiences, subjective time appears to slow down due to increased dopamine signaling. Think of how long vacations feel compared to stressful workdays.

By consciously repeating, "I have as much time as I think I do," women can shift from unease over things that may not unfold as planned, to trusting in the flow of organic opportunities ahead. Your mindset influences perceived time abundance. Reduce self-imposed pressures around linear ticking clocks. When at peace, your perception of time expands.

If you would like to learn more about aligning with time to ditch what you know about time management, you can take a class called "The Art of Timefulness: Making the Most of Life with the Time You Have." Visit https://ana-barreto.com/bonus.

Mental Stress Relief

Let's address self-criticism, lack of support, and workplace politics.

Stress often originates from unhelpful thought patterns like catastrophizing, perfectionism, rumination, and magnification. Women's imaginations are great for creativity, but often sabotage us into visualizing and expecting the worst. It takes the same effort to expect the worst as it does to expect the best. Here are some techniques to calibrate your thoughts and create space for mental health

- **Leaving the job**: Learn when it's time to leave before you are forced to. Some workplaces don't deserve the presence of women.

Here is one of them: Patricia worked in a male-dominated industry. In her small company, there were only two women and about around thirty males. The other woman was a manager, and Patricia felt hopeful that she would help her navigate that environment. Patricia shared with me that her coworkers were sexists, ignored her comments, spoke over her, made inappropriate jokes, and more. Only the gay guys were nice to her. When Patricia complained to the female manager, her concerns were ignored. She realized that the female manager was "one of the guys."

Patricia needed the money and decided to just put her forty hours in and ignore the rest. The place was a revolving door. New workers would not stay any longer than the old ones. One day, one of the newbies made a big mistake at the production line where he was working by Patricia's side. Two of the male bosses called her into the office and ganged up on her, blaming her for the mistake. The two managers wouldn't let her talk, and all she wanted to tell them was that no one in the production line listened to her. She had coached the newbies before, but they would ask questions to someone else (right in front of her) who had been there less time than she had. Many times, the others were wrong. The managers wouldn't accept her explanation and wrote her up. Since that day, Patricia dreaded going to work. Her senses were overloaded. She was hyper-vigilant, expecting the next bad thing to happen. She wasn't sleeping well. She wanted to look for another job, but had no energy to do so at the end of the day.

Patricia's girlfriend told her that she looked sick and that no job should cause anyone that much harm. That day, Patricia went to the manager and quit. She gave two weeks' notice and worked her full shift. Patricia clocked out and went to her car. One of the bosses ambushed her in the parking lot when she was already inside the car. Patricia rolled down the window, "Don't bother coming in tomorrow," he said. She was frustrated but thought it was probably for the best. She turned the car off, opened the door to go back into the building to pick up her things, but he stopped her. "I will have someone get them for you." Patricia got back into the car and drove away crying, regretting all the days she worked on her days off and put up with the harassment at the workplace.

- **Clear your lenses**: If you wear lenses of victimhood, you will filter everything as a victim. The best way to clear your lenses is by asking yourself questions. Is this true? Is this true beyond reasonable doubt? Some business is not your business. Who cares what others say or think about you? Know your value. If you don't know your value, why would anyone else know?
- **Ask questions**: It's time to address what is important. Some questions will be confrontational but needed. If you don't understand, ask the question again and again until you understand.
- **Cognitive restructuring**: This entails identifying distorted negative thoughts and replacing them with balanced perspectives. Next time you catch yourself imagining the worst-case scenario, stop yourself and say out loud: "This is not what I want. I want …. (say the best scenario)"
- **Mindfulness**: Meditation, visualization, and staying present in the moment reduce fixation on hypothetical worries. However, it's easier said than done. To make it true to you, you need at least an eight-minute daily meditation. Start with guided

meditations for five to eight minutes and build it from there. Find my meditations at Ana-Barreto.com/Bonus.

- **Journaling**: Writing about emotions, challenges, and goals provides constructive reflection and release of pent-up feelings. Often, you will get into a flow and write down thoughts, feelings, and experiences you didn't know you had. It's like listening to yourself vent.

- **Learning**: Reading, attending classes, and listening to podcasts build confidence in managing leadership challenges through expanded knowledge. Every time you learn something new, it takes a bit of space in your brain. If they are not useful to you, you just create additional space for more. Also, when you become fascinated by something new, it takes your attention away from stress and helps you recover effortlessly.

In today's fast-paced, demanding world, practicing effective mental stress relief techniques is not just a luxury; it's an essential component of overall well-being. By making time to practice any of the suggestions above, we fortify ourselves against the relentless stressors of modern life.

Spiritual Stress Relief

This section will address Pressure to Conform and Discrimination.

If you experience repeated stress, this often signals misalignment between actions and core values. What you are doing contradicts what you want to do. Clarifying your deeper purpose and meaning provides direction. I have introduced a mindful practice to find clarity with my first book Women, Rice, and Beans. You can download this guided practice at Ana-Barreto.com/Bonus.

- **Set boundaries**: It's important to know when you or anyone else crosses the line, but you must first set the line. You need to know what you are willing to accept or resist. I think of boundaries as a lake. It's your lake, next to your lovely home. It has vegetation and marine life. Then others come and begin to drop things in your lake. You like it when they drop fish and frogs, but someone comes with a bag of garbage, and you decide to look the other way. Then someone else comes with an old rusty refrigerator. You get mad, but don't say anything. Then they come with an automobile. You must draw the line. Setting boundaries is like keeping your lake clean. Here are some ways to make that easier:

- **Know Your Values**: Women must identify their top values and assess whether their daily choices reflect the spirit of the life they plan to live, or if they will live someone else's.

- **Make Time for Reflection**: Busy women rarely carve out time for themselves. Taking contemplative walks or writing in a journal facilitates insight into meaning, priorities, and vision. Take a "Me Vacation." Schedule the time to be with yourself, without friends or family. Book a retreat, a weekend away or beach destination where you don't know anyone. "Me Vacations" are a great way to build your confidence, spend time with yourself, and reevaluate your life. You can use my "Soul Compass: A Journal for Intentional Living" to help you journal your thoughts and feelings on paper and be absolutely certain that you are living congruently. Schedule it, or it is unlikely to happen.

- **Emerge in Art**: Creative expression through painting, pottery, writing, or music awakens passion and joy. What brings you joy? Make it a part of your life.

- **Build Support Networks**: Prioritizing family time, friendships, and community sustains mental health. Set boundaries to protect and nurture your relationships.

- **Practice Self-compassion**: Women are the most compassionate beings to others. Be willing to be kind to yourself in the face of setbacks. Compassion starts with self-compassion, giving yourself the brakes you extend to others.

Preventing Burnout

In my second book, *Self-Trust: A Healing Practice for Women Who Do Too Much*, I shared my theory that "trusting the self" is the antidote for burnout. The underlying cause of burnout is a few mindsets that cause women to overthink, over feel, and overdo, causing them an incredible amount of stress that sneaks in unannounced, until it takes over their lives. Unmanaged stress accumulates damage over time. It starts with tiredness, exhaustion, and feeling overwhelmed, leading to burnout.

Burnout sabotages both leadership capacity and physical health. However, establishing stable support systems, boundaries, and early self-care practices prevents it. Many women ignore the signs of burnout. They have learned to push through.

The tell-tale signs of impending burnout include lack of energy, constant irritability, lack of motivation, withdrawal from responsibilities, and an eroded sense of purpose. Noticing those warning signs and promptly restoring balance keeps burnout at bay.

Sustainable Routines

Having daily habits that proactively moderate stress, nourish the spirit, prevent depletion, and keep the inspiration flowing are easy practices for women. Rituals provide anchors in tumultuous times. People crave comfort moments, and rituals provide them. Have you noticed that you crave hot chocolate when things are not up to par? Perhaps that's what your mother gave you when you were upset. Although dark chocolate offers great benefits for women by helping relax the muscles and uplift their moods without too many calories, creating healthy morning rituals that can be sustained will support Holistic Leaders to become their best selves.

Start with one simple, sustainable routine, and then you can add more as you feel ready. Here are mine:

1) **Meditate for at least eight minutes each day:**
    When you first wake up in the morning, you are in the alpha state. Before you get sucked into the day's worries, take at least eight minutes to meditate, by concentrating on your breathing or following a guided meditation to catapult your day into a magical one. Thirty minutes would be ideal, but eight is enough to receive the benefits of meditation. You can meditate at any time during the day. Still, the morning will take you into higher levels of consciousness where creative ideas are born, solutions to problems are available, guidance for all areas of your life is available, and intentional actions begin.

2) **Make your bed:**
    I mentioned this routine earlier. But this is one of the easiest routines to start.

3) **Drink two glasses of water:**
    This act of self-care is also an easy routine to start.

Other potential practices to build into routines:

- Exercise
- Share gratitude at mealtimes or when you see a bird or butterfly
- Journal
- Schedule evening family dinners
- Unplugging from technology one hour before bed
- Schedule weekend nature outings
- Plan regular date nights

Holistic Leaders embrace Discipline and Personal Commitment. They know that these rejuvenating rituals are steady sources of resilience. Even small daily acts of self-care renew energy to lead powerfully over the long term.

Stress is an inevitable part of leadership, but it doesn't have to be persistent or constant. Be committed to embracing stress and treat it as a short heat wave. It will pass. It has to pass. By caring for physical, mental, and spiritual needs, women leaders transform stress into a sustainable drive. Thriving under pressure becomes second nature.

CHAPTER ELEVEN

MASTERING THE BASICS (MANAGEMENT SKILLS)

*"Leadership is about making others better
as a result of your presence and making
sure that impact lasts in your absence."*
— Sheryl Sandberg

Y ou first must crawl before you can walk or run. You must master Management skills before you can fly high in leadership. By the same token, we can't talk about Holistic Leadership without addressing the foundation of Leadership, which begins with management.

Management provides the fundamental building blocks of organizational leadership. Mastering core management functions like planning, organizing, directing, and evaluating establishes a strong foundation from which to lead strategically.

This chapter will provide an overview of how women leaders can excel at these four key management areas to complement their vision and influence capabilities.

Management and Leadership

Management and Leadership, though related, involve distinct skill sets. Effective leaders blend both. Management consists of practical, operational functions:

- Planning
- Organizing
- Directing
- Controlling

It keeps organizations running smoothly.

While Leadership focuses more on strategic influence— setting direction, aligning people, motivating change, and innovating—Management keeps organizations running smoothly. Together, they drive growth.

Strong managers ensure efficient day-to-day operations. Strong leaders rally people around inspiring futures. Excelling at both makes women executive material.

I have worked with long-term managers who were weak in one or three of the four parts of management. Also, I found that organizations are too quick to teach managers the job and expect them to become leaders overnight, without a proper foundation.

The Four Functions of Management

Mastering four fundamental management functions—Planning, Organizing, Directing, and Evaluating—creates a foundation for leadership success.

Planning

Planning involves defining goals and detailing the necessary steps to achieve them through research, analysis, and expert input. Strong planning prevents wasted efforts.

Effective plans reflect analysis, forecasting, and stakeholder perspectives. They specify responsibilities and deadlines. Detailed planning coordinates collaboration.

Key planning skills include:

-   Setting SMART goals (Specific, Measurable, Achievable, Realistic, Time-bound)
-   Researching solutions and best practices
-   Anticipating obstacles and designing contingency plans
-   Mapping dependencies and critical paths
-   Balancing ideal and realistic timelines
-   Forecasting

Planning transforms visions into executable action plans. It converts intentions into well-formulated strategies.

Opportunities

I once asked a manager who had been in the position for a few years what his plan for the week was. He didn't have an answer. Then I asked him what he did last week to prepare for this week, and he said he had been sick for three days. When I looked deeper, I saw that the manager had done a fair amount of planning for the week in the two days he worked, but he didn't realize what he was doing was planning.

One of the biggest opportunities for improving management effectiveness is addressing the need for more knowledge and more effective planning. Planning is a critical foundation of management, yet it is often neglected or else conducted haphazardly. This lack of intentional, comprehensive planning leads to wasted efforts, misalignments, delays, and reactionary leadership. When chaos happens, that signals a lack of proper planning.

Detailed project planning identifies required steps, stakeholders, constraints, risks, and resources needed to optimize execution. Without this forethought, initiatives easily stall or fail to meet objectives. Strategic business planning gives direction and aligns various efforts. However, many organizations do annual but scattered planning and small businesses often do none at all. This leads to working at cross purposes.

Leaders often underestimate the time and detail required for robust planning. However, the biggest management opportunity is taking the time upfront to chart thoughtful plans and analyses. As the saying goes: "By failing to prepare, you are preparing to fail."

Everyone needs to plan for the year, month, week, and day. This is not excessive planning. Before arriving at work, you must have a plan for the day. On Monday, you need to have a plan for the week. At the end of the month, you need to have a plan for next month. At the end of the year, you need to have a plan for the following year. It seems like a lot, but it's not. This is the foundation that keeps the world of business going. If you are led by the wind, going in whatever direction situations take you, you won't go far. If you do get somewhere, it's dumb luck!

While planning may not seem glamorous, it is the secret ingredient for outstanding management and optimal results. Lack of planning sabotages more initiatives than anything. People have brilliant ideas that are killed by improper or no planning.

To become better planners, leaders must make the time to plan, review plans often, adjust, and ask for feedback. There are many roads to get to Rome, but here is one way:

The Road to Rome

Begin by looking at your plan for the year. If you work for medium—to large organizations, your leaders already have the strategy, which outlines how you will achieve the plan. If the plan was not communicated, ask for it. If your organization is flying by the seat of their pants, or it's your company, build a plan. Then, break the year into quarters. The stock market does it, why wouldn't you? Write down the list of actions that must happen in each quarter. To make these decisions, you need to research a bit. Then, break it down into months. Each month, list the actions that must happen that month. Before the month is over, plan the following month. On Mondays, plan your week. Each day, plan what needs to happen during the day.

You must write plans down. You can use a notebook, agenda, computer, or a phone. If you haven't done this before, begin slowly by planning your weeks and days. For example, on Monday, list five things you plan to accomplish during the week. These five things need to be related to your goal. Then ask yourself, "Will these five actions move me forward? If yes, then break the actions down into days. If not, change the action.

This doesn't mean that you will do one action on Monday and another on Tuesday. You may complete three actions in one day and leave Monday and Friday free for the surprises business often delivers. Visit your planner daily.

A few years back, the company I worked for came up with a whiteboard planning tool. The company had the goals for the year, and each manager would write one goal for the month on the whiteboard, based on the overall goal. The board was visible to all. At the end of each week, the managers reviewed their progress, and at the end of the month, they reviewed the results. That year, my teams reached more goals than in previous years.

Takeaway from the Whiteboard Planning tool:

1) People actively creating their goals are more likely to reach them
2) Reviewing the goals daily leads to achieving them

3) Reviewing other's successes lead people to work more focused
4) The group supported the people lagging behind their goals

MBTI© and Planning

Your personality type will give you glimpses of your planning preference skills. The MBTI© "J" Judging's are better at planning. They thrive with goals and plans. The MBTI© "P" Perceiving's tend to wing it more than planning, or not allocate enough time to plan. It doesn't mean our MBTI© Perceiving's can't plan; they just need to schedule the time and commit to it, preferably in the early part of the day. On the other hand, as conditions change, the MBTI© Judging's tends to resist changing the plans they spent hours working on, while the MBTI© Perceiving's quickly adapt.

Organizing

Organizing entails coordinating tasks, workflows, and team member responsibilities to optimize collaboration and productivity. The function of Organizing enables seamless execution. There is a better way to frame this: Systems. You must have systems in place for everything. If, every time a task is to be done, someone must re-invent the system, chaos will take over the organization.

Many people can live amid chaos, but they shouldn't. Systems need be set and used all the time, by everyone. As a Holistic Leader, you need to create the Systems and ensure they are adhered to.

Some thinkers believe that systems stifle creativity, perhaps in certain areas of the organization. However, systems are like brushing your teeth. If you let kids brush them at random, your dental bills would be very high. That's why we devise systems as routines.

Skilled organizing involves:

- Structuring teams and reporting relationships
- Defining roles and responsibilities clearly
- Designing efficient systems and processes
- Managing handoffs proactively
- Establishing communication rhythms and norms

All successful organizations have systems in place to operate efficiently and consistently. However, the true test of a system lies in its ability to adapt and evolve when faced with unexpected challenges. The problem arises when individuals deviate from established systems without a coherent plan, leading to confusion and disarray.

This fundamental need for responsive and agile systems was brought into sharp focus during the COVID-19 pandemic. Businesses across industries had to rapidly revise their operational models to comply with evolving health and safety regulations. The restaurant industry, in particular, faced an unprecedented disruption—transitioning to a takeout and delivery model within twenty-four hours. Within a matter of days, these establishments were forced to implement entirely new systems for order processing, food preparation, and customer service.

During this tumultuous period, the ability to swiftly adapt systems proved to be a defining factor in an establishment's success or failure. Within just three weeks of the shutdown, clear winners and losers emerged in the industry. Customers flocked to the restaurants that could seamlessly pivot to the new takeout model, providing accurate and timely orders. In contrast, others struggled with persistent errors, long wait times, and dissatisfied patrons. The crisis highlighted the importance of not only having robust systems in place, but also the ability to rapidly modify and adhere to those systems in the face of disruptive change.

Directing People

Directing People focuses on overseeing operations, providing feedback and support, and keeping people focused on priorities. Directing brings plans to life. This segment of Management 101 is all about the people. Since the disruptive 2020 COVID-19 shutdown, many companies have been struggling with this function of management.

Leaders complained that they couldn't find qualified staff. The few people they attracted had to be highly compensated compared to the people they had already been working with. Because they were short-staffed, the new hires were not trained properly and didn't learn the systems. Existing employees were overworked, frustrated, and overwhelmed with the new hires' lack of performance, and left. Companies were stuck with highly paid, untrained staff who didn't know the systems, were not engaged, and often upset the customers. Strong leaders also experienced the earthquake of staffing, but it was quickly corrected because of one thing: Team members had leaders they liked and respected.

When we invest time and effort in the second most important function of management, "Directing our people," we focus on five key areas with tremendous passion and commitment. However, it may be all irrelevant depending on your self-assessment of your relationship with people in general. Before listing the key areas, you must ask yourself the ultimate question:

How much do you love working with people?

On a scale from one to ten, one being not at all and ten being you are in love with them, and working beside them feeds you at your core, how much do you love your people? If you rated yourself seven or below, you need to stop and reflect on these two questions:

Is being a leader something you want to invest your time in? Why?

The workforce today requires an enormous amount of effort compared with forty or even just twenty years ago. The workforce today requires more tender loving care from leaders. People struggle to connect without technology, have difficulty hearing negative feedback, and experience anxiety at a higher rate than previous generations. These lovely people have higher expectations from their employers, and the need for fairness is their compass to staying or leaving immediately, even if their perception of fairness doesn't match the company policy they briefly reviewed during orientation. The evolution of the workforce is keeping leaders honest. You can't fake leadership these days. You are either a good leader, a new leader with potential, or a rotten one.

Key Areas of Directing

Effective leadership goes beyond simply delegating tasks and overseeing operations. True Leadership starts with Managers who master a multi-faceted skillset to inspire, align, and empower their teams to achieve sustainable success. In the ever-evolving business landscape, where change is the only constant, the ability to provide clear direction and guidance becomes paramount. Focus on these five main areas, and you will have a better journey than most.

1. **Recruiting:**
   The first key area of Directing is Recruiting. The new person you bring into your team can make or break your team's performance. Outside of the time and money spent training new hires, a bad hire brings down morale in organizations, which is often overlooked by managers, but not by leaders. Sourcing and selecting qualified candidates that fit the culture cannot be done with a five-minute interview cut short because you are understaffed. Model your hires based on successful team members and the qualities you need to do the work right and effortlessly.

   Also, remember this statistic: One top performer will uplift the performance of the people around by 15 percent. One poor performer will diminish the performance of his coworkers by 30 percent.

2. **Development:**
Once you hire the right candidate, making time for their training and development is essential. This is the second key area in Directing. Unfortunately, great employees are often overlooked because managers can't find their replacements to allow for advancement. These days, the best new hires want to speed up the company ladder and get to the highest position and salary available. Some companies have systems in place, while others fly by the seat of their pants. There is no scientific method for promotion, but one must remember that "We cannot microwave experience."

Some managers will speed up the process because they are afraid of losing great employees to the competition. However, this is an unwise move. Speed promotions could lead these high performers to lose themselves not far down the path. If they don't have most of the skills to fulfill the role or the perseverance and time to get there, they will not make it. Holistic Leaders create a mentoring program with set marks to evaluate progress and communicate the path and speed of the process.

3. **Motivation:**
The third area of Directing People is motivating them. People are motivated by different things. There is not one size fits all when we study motivation, but some leaders have been able to encourage people to do the job they are paid for contentedly "most of the time." Holistic Leaders inspire engagement and ownership through clarity, care, and recognition. People are not an employee identification number or a pawn in the corporate game. People want to be seen, heard, and recognized for their contributions, even if minimal.

The million-dollar question scholars are looking to answer is, "How do you motivate people?" I say the right question is, "When do you motivate people?"

Holistic Leaders are always looking for opportunities to see, hear, and let them know they matter, not only during reviews. Today's leaders are called to guide their people to a better life by giving feedback and suggestions, resolving conflict, connecting them with others who can help, and counseling them. These days, progress is as good as success, though some executives may disagree with me. However, if people cannot recognize progress, they are likely to give up, and you are back at step zero.

Pay attention to people who play sports competitively. They have the resilience we are looking for in business settings today. Although getting a trophy and ice cream when the team loses the game is a sign of friendship and camaraderie, it doesn't prepare individuals for the real world when we lose or get disappointed. But there is hope when you use the Theory of Elasticity.

The Theory of Elasticity

Use the Elasticity Theory when motivating others. Catch your best people doing well and progressing. Make a big deal about them, and others will follow. The theory of Elasticity considers the force between connected individuals. When you pull on the positive side of the spectrum, the people on the opposite side will respond toward the side being pulled. If you pour your attention on the underperformers, the top performers will respond too, but toward the underperformers.

4. **Empowerment:**
   The fourth area of Directing is empowering your people. The word Empowerment has been thrown around for a few decades now. "Let's empower our people," managers say. But what

does it really mean? By definition, it's the process of becoming stronger and more confident, especially in controlling one's life and claiming one's rights. It allows people who are closest to the customer to make decisions that will benefit all.

Carla, a manager for a busy restaurant, came up with a new system to sell more alcoholic beverages. Because she worked for a chain, her idea would be off-brand standards. The manager decided that they would do it every day, but when the district manager visited, they would hide it. The sales increased, and the district manager noticed the results. Feeling afraid that someone would spill the beans, Carla decided to come clean with the district manager. When he heard of her idea and validated her results, he was ecstatic and asked her why she would hide a great idea. Carla shared that the previous district manager told her not to do it because he believed it was cheating. All she'd done was to feature popular drinks in a postcard-size menu and have the hosts present it to the guests when they were seated.

When people feel they have to hide their decisions, there is a problem in management. Empowerment leads to high engagement and action, fostering autonomy, inclusion, and leadership opportunities. The manager, Carla, is a gem. Many women seldom take empowerment risks as she did. On a positive note, women are more likely to praise and motivate others naturally.

5. **Work-Life Integration:**
The fifth key to successful directing is to promote work-life integration. We cannot be considered good leaders if we don't fully engage in promoting work-life unification in the workplace, which simply means some days the work wins, and other days the personal life wins. Some days, the team member leaves early to watch their son's baseball game; some days, they stay late to cover a short-staffed shift.

At times, that requires managers to consider short-term loss for long-term gain, which is seldom adopted. The need for qualified and motivated employees has driven managers to rethink their decisions to overwork their teams because of short staffing. Workers don't want to resent their jobs. But long workdays, longer work weeks, dual jobs, lack of days off, and pressure for people to take overtime, can lead workers to burnout, and ultimately to leave the jobs they once loved.

Holistic Leaders have the responsibility to help the workforce manage their lives by promoting flexibility, work/life boundaries, and self-care.

Life-Work Integration starts by paying attention to your people. Most employees will not complain about being overworked or being the one who never calls out, stays late, and works on their days off. The ones who do complain will not be placed on a busy schedule because managers don't want to deal with their mouths. However, the ones not complaining will be the first ones to leave, and this could be prevented.

Evaluating

Evaluating is the fourth function of management, often called *Controlling*. It consists of monitoring results, tracking metrics, assessing performance, and identifying improvement opportunities. It ensures efforts remain aligned with goals. However, there is a new breed of managers who don't like looking at results. They claim there is a tremendous amount of pressure to do so, and they dread going to work because of it.

If this is you, please take three breaths before you read the next sentence.

**"It's not the results that are creating your
anxiety; it's the way you interpret them."**

It's not the results or the boss that are putting pressure on you, it's what you say to yourself after you read the results.

Chances are your inner critic is saying things like: "You suck," "You are going to be fired," "You are an imposter," and more. With this frame of mind, no wonder you don't want to see the results. Let's try something new.

If you are traveling from New York to California, don't you want to know that you are going in the right direction? It would be best if you went west and not south to Florida. You don't want to drive ten hours and find out that you are in South Carolina. Reports are like maps or a GPS. It tells you where you are, and the direction you are heading.

You can't "ostracize" your performance by ignoring the results. It's not productive. I've found three ways to improve a team's anxiety around reports and evaluations:

1) Change the way you think about reports. It's only a GPS. You don't get mad at the GPS when you take a wrong turn, right?
2) Find the progress in each metric, even if you need to look with a magnifying glass. There are many metrics to look at. Pay attention to the progress, and the compass will move—it has to.
3) Celebrate success and progress. Do not wait until the end of the quarter or year to celebrate successes, because you may not have any to celebrate. Do it daily, weekly, and monthly. That's what progress is all about. You are not there yet, but you are moving in the right direction. Find yourself catching positive changes, even in individuals, and celebrate.

When it comes to improving performance, the Theory of Elasticity is useful. Take a rubber band and hold it on each side with one hand. Now, use your other hand and pull each side apart. If both sides pull equally strongly in their direction, the rubber band will stretch and break. But if we pull on one side a bit stronger than on the other, the other side has to move. By placing all of your attention on the underperformers, you are not moving them in the right direction.

Holistic Leaders consistently inspect what they expect. They don't micromanage or measure performance by numbers alone. They know that people need time to improve, and evaluating where they are in relation to the final goal will anchor the right efforts to real outcomes.

The Holistic Leader knows how to make the best use of evaluation results. We don't ignore poor results and are not emotionally led by them. It's by working through this function of management that we turn around performance.

If a business is not delivering results, use the other three lenses to diagnose those results. Is poor planning to blame? Do we lack the proper systems? Do you have the right business model? How are the people doing, from team members to managers?

Over the decades, fundamental management abilities have remained relevant, while technical skills have become outdated. Leaders have evolved in their approach to management, but the fundamentals stayed the same. Holistic Leaders must invest in mastering these four basic pillars if they want to become leaders others want to follow.

Mastering the fundamentals of management provides women leaders the competence and confidence to execute the vision. With a strong operational foundation beneath them, they can build lasting legacies that tangibly improve lives. Holistic Leadership means both reaching for the horizon and understanding the terrain between it and where you are. When women hone their management basics alongside a high-level vision, they become unstoppable agents of change.

Overcoming Gender Stereotypes

Historically, management has been viewed as a masculine domain, favoring qualities such as strategic thinking, decisiveness, and directness, all traditionally seen as inherently male strengths. This has led to the biased perception that women lack the essential management building blocks.

However, research shows no meaningful differences between men's and women's inherent abilities in functions like planning, organizing, directing, and evaluating. The gaps often arise from a lack of opportunities, not a lack of capability. With equal access to management development and experience, women excel.

In fact, many women leaders leverage stereotypically feminine strengths like collaboration, nurturing, and multi-tasking to their advantage in management roles. Their diverse perspectives strengthen organizations. Handling promotions based on competence, not gender stereotypes, ensures that all management talent is fully leveraged.

With this, we conclude the key principles of mastering the fundamentals of leadership. The subject is vast and requires additional learning, which you should continue on your own. In the next chapter, we will cover Stress Management, and the primary lifeline of women's success: self-care.

CHAPTER TWELVE

YOUR VALUES ARE YOUR COMPASS

"I believe great people do things before they are ready."
— Amy Poehler

There is an old fable about an elephant and a dog who were both pregnant at the same time. As neighbors, they would chat daily about their progress and growing bellies.

The dog gave birth after just three months and had a litter of cute puppies. A bit over three months later, the dog delivered another litter. But the elephant was only halfway through her gestation period. Despite not yet having her baby, the elephant was thrilled for her friend.

Over the following months, the dog grew curious as her own puppies grew up while the elephant remained pregnant.

Are you sure you are pregnant? Asked the dog to the elephant. Why was it taking you so long?"

The elephant calmly replied, "My dear, all pregnancies have their proper duration. If yours was two months, mine is twenty-two. Why compare us? Our journeys are different, but both beautiful in their own time."

Like the impatient dog, leaders undermine their serenity when fixated on others' timelines. Each has its own path and values to honor. Progress flows from inner purpose, not outer perception.

The ancient fable of the dog and elephant serves as a powerful reminder of the futility of comparison and the importance of focusing on one's own path. Just as the dog wasted its energy, leaders can become distracted by constantly measuring themselves against others, losing sight of their authentic goals and capabilities.

While the tendency to compare oneself to others is a universal experience, societal pressures and ingrained narratives can exacerbate this tendency, particularly for women in leadership roles. Rather than succumbing to the trap of constant comparison, true growth emerges when we turn our gaze inward, cultivating self-awareness and aligning our actions with our core values and aspirations. Plus, no women come out as winner when they compare themselves to others.

When we clarify and connect with our personal values, we strengthen our true intentions and find the courage to navigate challenges with unwavering confidence. This chapter explores how this process of self-discovery and value alignment can liberate women leaders from the shackles of comparison, empowering them to chart their unique course with authenticity and resilience.

Guiding Coalition

Our values represent the ideals and causes that matter most to us and the organizations we choose to serve. They are the guiding lights for our behaviors and decisions.

Personal values reflect deeply held convictions like integrity, growth, creativity, love, justice, wisdom, courage, freedom, or service. They stem from our upbringing, culture, beliefs, and our conclusions from life experiences.

It's not a surprise that shared values bind teams and organizations. However, when we bundle a group of people into an organization, we find that they come from different backgrounds, countries, religions, and political views. We can still align them by steering them toward company principles like excellence, inclusion, sustainability, innovation, accountability, community, and ethical conduct. Having clear personal and organizational values helps leaders and their people distinguish beneficial pursuits from hollow achievements. The process starts outside of work.

A 2020 study published in the Journal of Higher Education Policy and Management found that 71 percent of soon-to-be graduates said having an impact on society was just as important or more important than salary considerations. The study showed the need for leaders to vigorously communicate and live out their values and those of the organization. You can't assume everyone knows the mission as well as you do.

Ted, the CEO of a large corporation, visited a number of facilities and asked new and mid-level managers if they knew about the company's mission. Very few people knew the answer. How can leaders be aligned with the company mission if they don't know what the company stands for?

For leaders with strong personal values, there is a sense of purpose and serenity in the decisions they make. But these brilliant leaders were not always there. It all began with one question many people dare not ask.

Take your journal out and walk through the process by answering the following questions:

What do you want to do with the rest of your life?

Think about this question for at least ten minutes before answering the additional questions below that will support your clarity and help you decipher your mind and heart.

Many people are unable to answer this question, though it's the number two question humanity asks of everyone. The number one is "Why do I exist?", in case you want to know. Write your answer or thoughts out on paper.

Now, write down a list of your personal values. Try to find at least fifteen values. You are assembling your *"Guiding Coalition"* of values to direct future choices.

Don't stop until you find fifteen values that speak to you. Some people are either unaware, too afraid to find out if they belong elsewhere, are playing small, or are misaligned with their values. Now is the time to learn if you have been drinking coffee while preferring tea, just because you need to fit in.

My Value Coalition: Priority

1. _____ ( )
2. _____ ( )
3. _____ ( )
4. _____ ( )
5. _____ ( )
6. _____ ( )
7. _____ ( )
8. _____ ( )
9. _____ ( )
10. _____ ( )
11. _____ ( )
12. _____ ( )
13. _____ ( )
14. _____ ( )
15. _____ ( )

After you complete your list, consider these three points:

1) Prioritize the items on the list.
2) Pay attention to the last five items. There live the golden nuggets because they are usually hidden deep in your heart. Have courage and investigate them further.

3) Revisit and refine your list regularly as your self-knowledge deepens.

Prioritizing Values

Upon reflection, a hierarchy of values emerges. After doing the work, women leaders often realize the tradeoffs, compromises, and competing values are out of alignment with themselves.

For instance, valuing career achievement, family, and knowledge leads to different choices than elevating freedom, sustainability, and friendship. There are no right or wrong answers, only authentic priorities.

Once you have a clear list of your Value Coalition, rank them in order of Importance. Then, evaluate how your daily choices align with them. Not making a choice, or having it be made for you, is still your choice. Are your values and actions congruent? Where do conflicts arise?

Periodically re-evaluating and re-ranking your values is a crucial practice for sustained personal growth and alignment. As we evolve and encounter new experiences, our perspectives and priorities naturally shift over time. By intentionally reassessing your values on an annual basis, you create a ritual that fosters self-awareness and ensures your actions remain congruent with your deepest motivations.

Setting an annual evaluation around significant milestones, such as your birthday, the start of a new year, or the onset of spring, can be particularly impactful. These transitional periods instill a mindset of renewal and introspection, making them ideal times to recalibrate your value hierarchy. This exercise not only helps you maintain clarity amidst competing values but also promotes a dynamic and honest dialogue with yourself. Through this process, you gain the insight necessary to realign your choices with your ever-evolving sense of purpose, ensuring that your decisions and endeavors remain authentic expressions of your true self. An annual values reassessment acts as a powerful anchor, grounding you in your core principles while allowing for the natural evolution that accompanies personal growth.

Aligning Work and Personal Values

Leadership offers rich opportunities to enact values. However, toxic environments force compromise on ethics, which breeds misery. When leaders ignore their inner wisdom in favor of status or approval, integrity suffers.

Consider the recent ethical lapses at Wells Fargo Bank. Driven by toxic incentives emphasizing sales growth above all else, employees faced pressure to open fraudulent accounts without customer consent. This culture eroded integrity at all levels. Dishonesty ran amok in an environment that corrupted employees' lack of self-awareness. When people fear losing their jobs, they are likely to behave outside their values, if the values are not clear.

A Holistic Leader would have paused to question whether such aggressive sales goals truly honored deeper organizational values of honesty, transparency, and exceptional customer service. By fostering an environment of open dialogue, they could have empowered employees to voice concerns and realign priorities. However, the allure of outsized profits may have led many to rationalize unethical behavior. Holistic Leaders must create psychologically safe spaces where ethical dilemmas can be openly discussed. It's important for moral courage to be celebrated over blind obedience to policies that may violate core principles.

In the end, Wells Fargo paid billions in fines and settlements, facing immense reputational damage. When work environments force choices between ethics and rewards, it damages both organizations and the individuals within them, eroding their sense of integrity and self-worth. Holistic Leadership means having the courage to uphold moral principles, regardless of potential accolades or financial gains promised by compromising one's values.

If leaders find themselves in environments where they are being asked to violate ethical codes of conduct, they must reflect deeply on whether that organization aligns with their personal values. Holistic Leaders are the prime assets of organizations, and if companies fail to value and nurture those assets, it may be time to make the difficult decision to part ways. True leaders do not simply resign themselves to unethical practices, but actively work to transform organizational cultures or seek out environments that resonate with their moral foundations.

Always assess whether your organizational values and culture reflect your personal priorities. If current work conflicts with your conscience, either build coalitions to shift the culture or seek new opportunities. That inner discord will not go away—it will stifle your potential and kill your creativity. No one wants to be where they don't feel appreciated or have the room to contribute. If you truly believe change can happen, recruit a team with mutual values to amplify the changes you seek with impact.

Mother Teresa said, "None of us, including me, ever do great things. But we can all do small things with great love, and together, we can do something wonderful."

Setting Boundaries

Boundaries are the silent architects of healthy relationships, including the one between you and yourself. I have encountered too many women not setting boundaries, setting but ignoring them, or allowing them to be too loose. Well-understood values make for well-established boundaries.

Clear boundaries are the key to well-being. In the rush of responsibilities, women often overextend by blending work, family, self-care, and more, until none of it gets the focus it deserves. Divided energy breeds exhaustion, ineffectiveness, and burnout over time. The solution is simple: know your limits and learn to set firm boundaries.

Boundaries entail consciously defining and communicating reasonable lines based on values, capacities, and personal needs in the areas of time, relationships, finances, workload, and more. They help preserve space for self-care, prevent energy drain, and reduce endless multitasking.

You cannot sustain giving to others without first filling your own cup. Make strengthening boundaries around physical, mental, and emotional well-being a priority.

You have already listed your core values and assessed your current alignment. Are you living someone else's priorities instead of your own? If so, categorize where you feel depletion occurring. Is it physical fatigue? Financial strain? Relationship imbalance? Emotional toll? Spiritual crisis? Pinpoint specifically where stronger boundaries would help avoid depletion.

Women have learned to produce at all costs, using exorbitant amounts of willpower. Just because you can overextend yourself doesn't mean that you should.

Next, determine what requests you can reasonably say no to, and where you must set firmer limits on things like working hours, volunteer commitments, insensitive friends, and purchases.

At first, it's important to draft a kind but concise language to reinforce those lines, like "No." That is a complete sentence, and perfectly acceptable. "No, thank you," is another complete sentence. Refrain from explaining, but if you must, use "I cannot take that on right now."

Women tend to explain too much, especially if they haven't honored their limits before. You don't owe anyone explanations. The people who are used to counting on you will need to find additional help to take on your large workload. Practice saying: "Thank you for thinking of me, but I cannot (do, commit, give) right now." *Please do not ask them to check back with you later!* That's your saboteur talking.

Finally, honor these new boundaries unapologetically. Others will test them, so stay strong and redirect repeated requests instead of caving in. Your new communication is based on self-care, not selfishness. You cannot serve at your highest potential while running on empty due to a lack of boundaries.

You are not required to meet every demand placed on you. Women must unlearn cultural conditioning and stop being endlessly pliable people-pleasers. Your needs matter too. Practice the courage to honor them.

When your boundaries are tested, repeat yourself two or three times until the other person hears it. "I understand this project is important, but I already have several critical deadlines on my plate." "Like I said, I understand this project is important, but I already have several critical deadlines on my plate." You don't need additional explanations.

This doesn't mean that you refuse all requests for help. There may be additional projects at work that will enhance your abilities or additional responsibilities that have a potential for growth. This is about your self-care. I encourage you not to run your life on empty. No one will benefit from it.

By aligning actions with authentic priorities through boundaries, you fill your cup first so you can give from abundance, not depletion. Self-care enables better care for others in the long term. Prioritize strengthening boundaries around your well-being starting today—you are worth it!

Navigating Trade-offs

By now, you may have found that not all of your competing responsibilities align perfectly with relative values. Inevitable trade-offs require additional reflection for clarity. When facing dilemmas, reflect on higher-level values being upheld or betrayed with each option. Look at your Value Coalition and assess which choice aligns with your core self, even if imperfectly.

Also, consider which option has the potential to cause regret. Will passing on a promotion to have another child later create resentment? Would leaving a secure job for an unproven startup prompt anxiety? Before you weigh short and long-term alignment, know that:

*"Every decision is the right decision based on the
level of consciousness you have at that time."*

Copy the statement above and post it in your office, bathroom, phone notes, or bedroom. Impeccable choices are impossible. The goal is to make decisions that will bring you more fulfillment. You can always correct the trajectory as more wisdom arises from experiences.

CHAPTER THIRTEEN

CONFIDENCE AND COURAGE MATTERS

*"If there's a book you really want to read, but it
hasn't been written yet, then you must write it."*
— Toni Morrison

In this chapter, you will learn four techniques to help you build your confidence and courage, and use them when you need them.

Lack of confidence is the number one issue for women. A Hewlett-Packard internal study found that women only apply for open jobs if they think they meet 100 percent of the listed qualifications, while men apply if they meet just 60 percent.

According to an ABC News/Washington Post poll in 2018, 56 percent of women reported that lack of confidence was a major element holding them back. Only 29 percent of men agreed with that statement.

In 1992, when I was beginning my career, I shared with a male coworker that I used to have more confidence when I was younger, living in Brazil. He asked me why, and I told him that I felt people thought I was stupid. I had an accent, mispronounced words all the time, and hadn't completed my college degree. The following day, he gave me an unopened cassette audiobook from Jack Canfield, titled *How to Build Self-Esteem*. His high school coach had given it to him. He was already in his mid-twenties, and he had never used it. The program was amazing, and I learned to reframe my mindset. Since then, I have bought the same program to share with others I felt might benefit from Canfield's work.

As I built my teams, I found that about 90 percent of the women I worked with lacked confidence. There were males on the team too, but they were mainly African Americans and Hispanics. The lack of confidence came across as they brought their weakness to the spotlight in conversations, put themselves down, and doubted their decisions, even though they had succeeded before. Women stayed quiet when they were disrespected, ignored confrontations, lied when they made an honest mistake, passed their decisions off to others, choked in interviews, sabotaged their opportunities, and walked away from promotions to stay underemployed. The most disheartening was when women didn't put their name in the hat when they were the most qualified candidates, giving up on their ambitions for fear of disappointment.

If you have experienced any of the situations above or know someone who has, please know that you can overcome them, starting now. Remember to bring your umbrella.

Confidence is often confused with courage. Though related, courage and confidence have distinct meanings with significant overlap. Confidence entails assuredness in one's abilities and a sense of self-efficacy, taking action without insecurity or self-doubt. Courage represents emotional strength, enabling one to face hardship, adversity, uncertainty, or intimidation, without giving in to fear.

Courage often springs from confidence. When you know your talents and worth, it empowers courageously standing up for yourself and the truths you believe in. Self-assurance steels the nerves and builds bravery. Courage also reciprocally builds confidence through perseverance, despite fear and anxiety.

I find that confidence is 50 percent preparation and 50 percent mindset. So is courage. Women tend to spend their entire time preparing for a role, learning all the ins and outs of a job, mastering the mechanics, and forgetting their mindset. Women need to dissect the thoughts they need to keep, adjust, or release. These thoughts will guide their emotions and actions when it matters.

Everyone is born with confidence and courage, with no exceptions. You may be asking, "Then where is mine?", It's inside of you. Over the years, incidents have happened that led you to feel a lack of confidence and courage. But the golden nugget is there, inside of you, waiting to be rediscovered. You will need to unlearn some of the safety mechanisms your mind created as a precaution against the suffering you expected. You formed some of those thoughts on your own by building conclusions that met your needs at that time. Now, they have the potential to sabotage you as you become a Holistic Leader.

Here are my Confidence Exercises:

1) **Improve Your Body Posture**
   Stand up and feel as if you are a confident person. Close your eyes and see yourself as confident. Take three deep, slow breaths, breathing in through your nose and out through your mouth, and feel a bit more confident. Imagine how it feels to be *very* confident. Now, take another three breaths and feel a bit more confident than before. Notice your body, your shoulders, and your back. Repeat this exercise daily until you notice you can feel your confidence. Your body needs to feel what it is like to be confident, until it becomes a way of being. Please don't ignore this great mind-body hack—it works! Practice daily for at least thirty days. One mistake people make is to do the exercise on the day they have something important to do. It would be best if you built your confidence muscle gradually, until it becomes a natural habit.

2) **Practice Self-efficacy**
   Self-efficacy is the perceived capability of performing or achieving goals at a designated level. You can improve your perceived capabilities by changing your self-evaluation about achieving,

reviewing your past success to remind you of your accomplishments, modeling the behavior of other successful people, or working with an uplifting team. Later in this chapter, you will learn more about self-efficacy.

3) **The Law of Sympathetic Resonance**
Sit comfortably, relax, and close your eyes. Now, imagine sitting across a table from yourself. Look at her posture, eyes, dress, smile, and feel her energy. She is very confident. Pay attention to her arms, hands, and fingers. Notice her legs and feet. Feel how confident she is.

Now, step out of yourself and into that confident person. How do you feel? Notice how you feel the feeling of being confident for at least sixty-six seconds.

Open your eyes and feel the resonance of being confident for another sixty-six seconds.

Close your eyes again and imagine yourself sitting across from you. This time, the person across from you is more confident than before, perhaps 25 percent more confident. Sense her confidence.

Now, imagine yourself stepping into that person. Step out of yourself and into that confident person. Feel what it's like to be 25 percent more confident for sixty-six seconds. Notice how you feel being 25 percent more confident. Stay there for at least sixty-six seconds.

Repeat this exercise daily so your body knows how to feel confident and grow synaptic connections in your mind to be instantly confident when needed.

4) **Stop "Faking It Until You Make It"**
The concept of "fake it till you make it" suggests that if you pretend to be confident, eventually, real confidence will follow. This was a popular saying in the 80s, but in the 2020s, inauthentic acting has higher risks and consequences. Research shows

that successful leadership requires demonstrating genuine confidence stemming from capabilities and self-efficacy.

First, women leaders especially, may receive pushback or criticism if perceived as inauthentic or overly assertive. Studies show powerful women still face backlash for acting outside expectations. Rather than pretend, it is more sustainable to systematically build new capabilities and track records until real confidence emerges. You don't have to be 100 percent ready to succeed.

Second, leaders who "fake" competence rather than pursuing mastery risk failing themselves and others who depend on them. No one wins if responsibilities are given to someone who does not have the skills. Remember, leadership is about serving; becoming a fully confident, integrated leader is not about acting, but focused persistence in expanding skills.

Ultimately, leadership requires bringing your real, whole self to work. The most impactful, inspiring leaders have the emotional intelligence to understand their real strengths and growth areas, along with self-awareness to continue developing new capabilities over time. Rather than faking confidence, pursuing genuine self-efficacy in the unique combination of your values, vision, and abilities paves the sustainable path to leadership success.

If you would like to learn more about confidence and be supported during your journey, visit the Body, Mind & Wisdom School at www.bmwisdom.org and take the class "A Crash Course in Confidence."

Understanding Self Efficacy

In a 1989 study on Self-Efficacy, psychologists Hackett and Betz found that women consistently exhibit lower perceived self-efficacy than men in career roles, even when their actual competence was equal or greater.

Women majoring in male-dominated fields like engineering showed the bluntest confidence gap.

Basically, before taking one little action, women expect to do worse than they will really do. The biggest problem with this thinking is that it creates a self-fulfilling prophecy. Without intervention, women hesitate to take on advancement opportunities, ceding ground to possibly less competent but more *confident* men.

Let's Assess Your Self Efficacy by taking this quick self-assessment:

0 = Not confident at all
5 = Moderately confident
10 = Highly confident

Rate yourself in each question:

a) How confident are you that you can earn $100,000 next year?

                                                  _____

b) How confident are you that you can earn $200,000 next year?

                                                  _____

c) How confident are you that you can earn $300,000 next year?

                                                  _____

d) How confident are you that you can earn $500,000 next year?

                                                  _____

It's very likely that your self-rating started high and declined as the salary increased. Measuring self-efficacy is important because it predicts achievement and performance. If you don't believe it's possible, you are likely to meet your expectations. Self-efficacy is a high predictor of success, or the lack thereof, and an important key for building confidence in leadership.

There are four main ways to build self-efficacy: Mastering Performances, Social Modeling, Social Persuasion, and Improving Physical and Emotional States.

1. **Mastering Performance**: The best way to achieve high self-efficacy is by looking at your past successes. When you acknowledge your track record and celebrate it, you are more likely to look at new opportunities, take on new challenges, and stick with them until success is achieved. Each mastery experience builds evidence that you can do hard things. Conversely, if your past performance was below par, you are likely to have low self-efficacy. However, people tend to focus on negative events and struggle to remember the good things. Make a list of your top 10-15 achievements and save it.

2. **Social Modeling**: This involves seeing other similar people succeed, which inspires the belief that you can, too. Identifying other women who have done it is the first step that may lead you to try. The case I shared in chapter eight about posting the goal on a whiteboard builds self-efficacy. As everyone can see the wins and losses, it becomes a great example of social modeling. If other people are achieving their goals, you can do it too. Make a list of successful women you admire and save it.

3. **Social Persuasion** provides encouragement from others that you have the capability to succeed in leadership. This is the key to becoming a great leader. Helping people see their potential and coaching them during the process helps them build confidence and deliver results. The opposite can happen too. If a leader keeps pointing to the misses of every performance, the confidence level of the team can decline, even though they have the potential to succeed. Find 3 people to provide honest encouragement,

4. **Physical and emotional indexes** can help create mental readiness to take on new challenges or destroy them. Anxiety and stress are the ones on the top of the list.

I did a team-building exercise with a group of four managers who began working together less than three months before the beginning of the fiscal year. We did an exercise where they rated their self-efficacy

(SE) in reaching their individual goals. Two of the managers were female and rated their self-efficacy as seven of ten. They were new in their positions, and one of them was new to management. The third was a male manager and the most veteran in the group, who rated his SE as a six. He felt he'd had a weak performance in the previous year and would take some time to recover. The last manager rated himself as ten. He was new to his role, but he had always reached his goals in the past. We debriefed the results. The lower rated manager wanted to avoid the disappointment of not meeting their targets, but within a month of their meeting, the team's results improved. They finished the year with the three managers reaching their goals. The manager with the lowest efficacy of six improved, but didn't reach his goals.

In addition to the four methods above, developing a growth mindset, grit, resilience, and a learning orientation supports self-efficacy. With a growth mindset, women can reframe experiences like failure or criticism as opportunities to learn rather than as statements about fixed abilities. Grit involves persevering toward long-term goals despite challenges and setbacks along the way.

About Courage

Courage requires a level of conviction that cannot be described, only felt. Cultivate courage through spiritual practices like prayer, meditation, visualization, and affirmations to tap into an authentic power greater than any circumstance. Many have unlocked their courage by anchoring in timeless universal values like love, justice, freedom, peace, and humanity, and you can do it too.

My favorite case happened in 1977, when a sixty-three-year-old grandmother rescued her grandson from under a parked car. She lifted the Buick with one hand and pulled the child to safety with the other. Did she need her courage to lift the car? You'd better believe it. If anyone had asked her if she could lift a Buick that weighed about three and a half thousand pounds before the incident, she would undoubtedly have denied it. But the confidence was inside of her all along, and her courage was instantly ignited by the love for her grandson to pull him to safety. Again, confidence and courage are inside of you. You just need to have a compelling reason to harvest its potential.

In the end, you need to stay faithful to the voice of inner wisdom, whatever the cost, to build undisputable courage. The Universe rewards courage.

The Opposite side of Confidence

Pay attention to the distractions you create. It's easy for leaders to obsess over what peers, competitors, and experts are or aren't doing. But comparing themselves to others pulls focus away from their own objectives. This is one of the consequences of a lack of confidence.

The only metrics that matter are one's own goals and values. Leaders undermine their power when distracted by what fills other people's plates, and this includes gossip. Know that people have different trajectories, and wasting your time on other people's results is only fueling your lack of confidence.

With confidence and courage combined, women leaders can powerfully use their voice for change, pioneer new initiatives despite uncertainty, handle criticism resiliently, and expand their influence by conquering fear-based hesitation. Look for opportunities to flex both courage and confidence muscles simultaneously to maximize leadership growth. Feel the fear and do it anyway!

In the next chapter, we will cover how to build your alleys as a Holistic Leader.

CHAPTER FOURTEEN

BUILDING YOUR NETWORK OF SUPPORT

*"Never limit yourself because of others' limited
imagination; never limit others because
of your own limited imagination."*
— Mae Jemison

L eadership can be a lonely endeavor without a diverse network offering mentorship, sponsorship, problem-solving, and community. Thoughtfully cultivating connections multiplies your impact and potential for growth. This chapter provides strategies to build valuable support ecosystems.

A Holistic Leader must build their circle of women. You need to assemble a group of six to eight women to create your Circle of Brilliance, also known as the Circle of Authentic Women. These are the women you will call to ask for help and support. It could be considered a mastermind group, but it is free and based on a common alliance to further everyone's brilliance.

The Circle of Brilliance doesn't require meeting attendance, touching basis every week, or signing a group agreement, though I would encourage you to meet monthly. The women in your circle are probably already on friendly terms with you. They are people you called in the past for help, or who have called upon you. They are women you already know, admire, trust, and want to connect with when possible. They are not perfect, but they are real. All you need to set up your network is to contact them.

Forming a Circle of Authentic Women provides community, empowerment, and wisdom. This circle of trusted peers uplifts its members to actualize their potential through support.

It's like assembling your own "board of directors" with unique expertise. Include a sage mentor, candid friend, innovative peer, domain expert, dependable sponsor, organizational adviser, confidant connector, and even a personal listener.

In your Circle of Brilliance, you can pose challenges for solutions; drawing on the group's combined wisdom. You can reach out to each of them individually for dinner or coffee. You can add or rotate members as needed, based on your leadership journey. But first, you need to establish depth through vulnerability, trust, and mutual commitment. Invest in the relationships as well as the advice.

These days, many women are members of social media groups without participating. They like the group and read occasional posts, but don't contribute.

When selecting members for your Circle of Brilliance, seek women who exemplify qualities like:

- **Honesty** - Willing to share hard truths with care
- **Supportive** - Listens and validates you without judgment
- **Trustworthy** - Keeps confidence and has your back
- **Open-minded** - Brings creative solutions, not just complaints
- **Motivating** - Inspires you to keep progressing
- **Coaching** - Draws out your best self with compassion
- **Knowledge** - Offers expertise to tackle shared problems
- **Alignment** - Helps you see yourself in the mirror

A diverse Circle of Brilliance provides you with advisors, confidants, collaborators, and soul sisters. Again, you could meet regularly if you like, but it's not required. Smaller circles are easier to manage and participate in. I found that six to eight people is the ideal number for me, but you are free to explore larger or smaller groups.

Begin founding your Circle of Brilliance. List the women you already can count on and those you would like to add.

1. _____
2. _____
3. _____
4. _____
5. _____
6. _____
7. _____
8. _____

If you can't think of eight women to invite to your circle, don't add names just to complete the task. The right woman will show up in time. You also need to be available to be part of other circles.

Here is a sample letter to invite women to join your Circle of Authentic Women:

> *Dear [Name],*
>
> *I hope this email finds you well. I wanted to reach out because I am forming a Circle of Authentic Women, a small group of trusted peers who uplift each other through unconditional support, wisdom, and empowerment. This is a suggestion from the book, The Umbrella Effect: A Journey of Self-Mastery for Women Leaders.*
>
> *This circle aims to provide an open, judgment-free space where we can discuss our dreams, challenges, and victories as women seeking to live and lead authentically, and find solutions to our problems. By coming together in*

vulnerability, we can gain strength, insight, accountability, and sisterhood.

I immediately thought of you as someone I would be honored to have in my circle. You exhibit qualities like honesty, compassion, open-mindedness, trustworthiness, and positivity that would enrich my life. Your perspective and presence would be invaluable, and I am making myself available to you should you choose to create your own Circle of Brilliance.

If you feel aligned with the intention of this circle, I would love for you to join. There are no formal meetings, just individual check-ins as needed. We can call each other anytime we need support, guidance, advice, and to share our successes.

Please let me know if you are interested in learning more or joining my circle. I appreciate you so much and look forward to your response.

Warmly,
[Your Name]

Who are the Women to Consider for Your Circle of Brilliance?

Seek Mentors

Mentors provide knowledge transfer, counsel, and growth opportunities. They share wisdom forged through experience. You can target respected leaders who are succeeding through authenticity. Assess potential fits based on shared values, personality chemistry, and leadership styles. A mentor's living example should inspire you.

Cultivate Sponsors

While mentors advise, sponsors advocate. They leverage reputations to create advancement opportunities. Sponsors nominate protégés for key assignments, promotions, boards, speaking engagements, and funding. Their ringing endorsement opens doors for others.

Earn sponsorship through excellent work. Be sure to demonstrate skills, drive, judgment, and teamwork. It's not rude or conceited to share your accomplishments with people who could be your sponsor. Ask sponsors to invite you into their networks and recommend valuable training. When sponsors extend opportunities, they over-deliver on their expectations. Make them look wise for believing in you. Share credit and celebrate joint success, but avoid feeling entitled. Ingratitude erodes all forms of goodwill. Show readiness first, then patience. Your turn will come.

Embrace Initiative

When forming a group, be open to newbies: women starting their journey who have less experience than the rest of group. See them not as holding the group back, but as slowing it enough to help the group view the world from a beginner's perspective.

In 2013, I got invited to become part of a Mastermind Group of Women. The group was comprised of five businesswomen with five to thirty years of experience, and me, the new writer who was employed and beginning to build a nebulous dream of running my own business. It was a free mastermind group. I was writing my first book, and the other women were looking to scale their businesses and get guidance and support from one another. They were also older than me. During those ten months of attending the mastermind, I achieved more of my goals than in the years before. Even though I was the newbie and learned a lot from them, I also helped the group with time management, sales, systems, and accountability. Often, I was the only one who completed the assignments, shared the bits they didn't read, and offered spiritual support when they were overwhelmed.

Women's circles work!

Pay it Forward

Back in 1992, my Marketing Professor told me to get into the Sales Department if I hoped to build a career in Marketing. Reluctantly, I took his advice and went to the Human Resources Department to inquire about open sales roles.

Fortunately, the HR manager, Bridget, was dedicated to bringing more diversity into the sales team. She patiently coached me on how to ace the upcoming interview with the Sales Director. Bridget devoted hours prepping me on how to confidently answer likely questions, what professional dress would make the best impression, and how to conduct myself during the interview.

Thanks to Bridget's generous guidance, I landed the job! Her mentorship didn't stop there. She later went above and beyond again, diligently preparing me to be accepted into the company's Manager in Training program.

I'm forever grateful to Bridget for selflessly sharing her wisdom and empowering me to succeed as a young minority woman entering corporate leadership. She exemplified what it means to nurture talent and build clear pathways for others. So today, I take the time to coach everyone interviewing for entry and high-level positions who asks me for help. Thanks to Bridget, I pay her kindness forward.

Building Connections

Successful relationship-building requires both skill and a mindset shift. We must move from transactional encounters to the service of others. Here are some tips to secure strong networks:

- Frequently greet people by their names, either in person, via email, or even text. It signals care, and people simply like to hear their names.
- Be present and listen fully, without multi-tasking. Make genuine eye contact. Honor others' time. Many women, when they feel intimidated, tend to plan their response before they hear the question. Trust your sincere intention to be present and contribute.
- Show interest by asking thoughtful questions. Celebrate others success and progress. Follow up on previous conversations and try to initiate outreach.
- Offer help without expecting reciprocity. Always share knowledge, contacts, and credit, and be mindful not to be the "know it all" person who no one can stand. You don't always need to be on top and one-up everyone else. Unfortunately, people in general tend to share experiences that position themselves as better or as worse than others. For example, when others share a great vacation, they returned from, be happy for them and avoid sharing your best vacation. This is their time. When they share a disaster, don't top theirs. The way to know if you should add to the conversations is by answering this question: Is this contributing or taking away from what was said? People who have confidence don't need validation.
- Maintain integrity and build trust through reliability, honesty, and respecting secrets. Many female leaders share connections by revealing too much information about others. Please don't. If you over-extended yourself, be honest and break the agreement. It's better to confront your shortcomings honestly than ignore them or lie.

Relationship building is a marathon, not a sprint. If you value relationships and have a healthy degree of energy invested in building them, make the time to nourish and expand your networks. You can't receive what you don't give.

CHAPTER FIFTEEN

FIRE YOUR INNER SABOTEUR

"No one can make you feel inferior
without your consent."
— Eleanor Roosevelt

I'll always remember coaching my client, Lindsey, before an interview for a promotion. Despite being a successful manager with a stellar track record, she hadn't interviewed in years. While Lindsey oozed natural charisma, this was a high-stakes interview, and she needed to impress the executive panel. During three preparation sessions, we worked on honing her interview skills. She memorized a few key talking points to highlight her talents.

Yet, after the interview, a disappointed Lindsey called me. She confessed to being so nervous that she bombed it. She kept mumbling disjointed responses, forgetting the questions, and relying on memorized material that didn't actually answer what they asked.

A week later, the dreaded feedback came from her boss—Lindsey completely flubbed the interview. The executives noticed her extreme anxiety and even got her some water and gave her more time to help her calm down. Her paralyzing fear sabotaged all her hard work and stellar results. She didn't get the promotion.

Lindsey exemplifies how even the most accomplished leaders can sometimes succumb to imposter syndrome and anxiety. In those moments, inner brilliance gets drowned out by our inner critics whispering that we aren't good enough. Quieting those saboteurs is key to personal success.

Many women unconsciously undermine themselves, falling victim to the inner voices of self-doubt and unworthiness, despite their great talents. These imposters sabotage the confidence required to walk the leadership path. A woman may have done something numerous times successfully, but when someone is watching, she loses her self-assurance and flounders.

I believe these women have fallen victim to anxiety at the worst moment. Thoughts plagued them until they realized that those thoughts stemmed from flawed unconscious assumptions, not truth.

Most women have struggled with imposter syndrome. However, your confidence will grow once you trace those critical inner voices back to false narratives absorbed over time:

"I'm not qualified for that position yet."
"My ideas aren't valuable enough to share."
"I shouldn't brag about myself so boldly."
"I'm not good enough."
"I need more training."
"I have better results, but Pedro has been working longer than me."
"I can't take that much responsibility."

It's like someone is saying, "Who do you think you are?" If you are not sure, they will tell you what they think, and prove it to you by recalling every failure you have witnessed in yourself and others.

Do any of those internal scripts seem familiar? What helps you move past them is recognizing that those messages came from outside influences like sexism, early childhood experiences, lack of feedback and training, and cultural biases, not your own wise inner self.

That's good news. However, realizing that limiting beliefs are imposed externally doesn't automatically silence your inner critic. You need to actively reframe self-doubt into empowering perspectives, through daily practices.

You can't wait until the day before your big opportunity to do the work. The work starts today.

The anxiety and stress reactions that come from our inner critic are only trying to protect us by preventing us from leaving the safe status quo. But, no one is truly that unsafe. The following are three-morning practices that work with your mind, body, and spirit in unison to reprogram your subconscious and stop your actions of self-sabotage.

It takes only eight to ten minutes to complete them, but you may want to do it for a bit longer. Your brain might assume an exercise won't work because it's too short or too easy to be effective—again, this is your inner saboteur. Also, the mind could rationalize something so simple as being useless, but this really works when repeated.

Practice One: Body-Mind Connection

When you first wake up in the morning, sit in a chair. Close your eyes and feel the back of the chair. While feeling your back against the chair, take three slow, deep breaths and say to yourself, "I am safe." Breathe again and say, "I am safe." Breathe the third time and say, "I am safe."

Then, feeling your bottom on the chair, take three more deep breaths and say to yourself three times, "I am supported." Breathe. "I am supported." Breathe. "I am supported." Breathe.

Lastly, place your attention on your heart. Take three long, deep breaths and say to yourself, "I am an infinite being." Breathe. "I am an infinite being." Breathe. "I am an infinite being." Breathe.

This exercise creates a connection between the mind and the body, making you feel safe. When you feel safe, you can think clearly and take the appropriate actions you are being called to take.

Practice two: Self-Love Practice

Find a comfortable breathing pattern. Begin by rubbing your hands. Then, cross your arms and rest your hands on each shoulder. Then, begin by caressing both arms simultaneously, from shoulders to hands, while breathing deeply. Do it for at least sixty-six seconds. Feel the warmth and love you're extending to yourself. Say encouraging words to yourself, such as "I got you. You are doing great. I have your back. You are amazing. You are going to ace it. You can let go of that shit. You are ready; you have always been ready."

This simple act of self-nurturing builds the sense of being loved and appreciated, creating a fortress against anxiety.

Practice Three: Heart Anchoring

This exercise, besides firing your inner saboteur, is also a great practice to build self-efficacy.

Think of a moment in your life where you felt gratitude, happiness, and pride in yourself. Bring the event to mind. See yourself at that event. Remember how you felt. See in your mind what you were wearing. Go back in time and feel what you felt. Milk that moment. Feel the emotions as if you are there now. As you feel the amazing emotions, begin to tap on your heart area with your third and fourth fingers. Keep tapping for at least sixty-six seconds.

Think of another moment when you felt gratitude and immense happiness, then tap into your heart for sixty-six seconds. Do it again with yet a third memory.

This practice helps you build the emotions of success that can be recalled at any time by tapping on your heart in three sets of three. If you have an interview, need to do a speech, or need to make a strong impression, before doing it, tap on your heart to recall the right emotions, instead of past stress responses.

You can download these practices at Ana-Barreto.com/Bonus. I have added theta frequency music for faster results.

These practices work. With repeated effort, your true self-image will gradually rise. Your inner critic, over-protector, and saboteur will be silent, while your long-muted inner champion grows louder.

As your confidence expands, you'll feel inspired to take bold risks— have long overdue difficult conversations, apply for that big promotion, launch your business, and take an inspiring new initiative.

Once you trust your inner brilliance and allow it to shine without apology or disguise, the imposter syndrome loses its power. You'll realize success was inside you all along.

I recommend trying these simple but powerful practices to start silencing that inner saboteur. These three Mind Architects will help you physically change neural pathways to activate your confidence and evoke calm, so you can access what you need when you need it. You've got this!

Origins of Self-Doubt

It can be challenging for some female leaders to identify their thinking as the voice of the saboteur. This voice is often disguised by noble behaviors and ingrained in environments women frequent. Here are some of the bad seeds planted in those environments that have contaminated women's thinking.

- **Discrimination:** Women who were made to feel inherently unfit.
- **Perfectionism:** Women who grew up in an environment where "nothing was ever good enough."
- **Undue modesty:** Women who were discouraged from celebrating their success and encouraged to downplay their strengths and expertise.
- **Narrow self-concept:** Women who were compared to others and conditioned to identify tightly to achievement.
- **Attribution errors:** Women who were put down, discouraged, and learned to discount successes as flukes or luck.

In the path of rebuilding your confidence and silencing your saboteur, women need to be aware of these influences. Self-limiting narratives were imposed on them, not the truth. Left unaddressed, self-doubting thoughts become a self-fulfilling prophecy. People who doubt their worth hold themselves back and rise only to the level someone imposed on them, which is much lower than their full potential.

Stop Feeding the Imposter Syndrome

Women are natural givers, and one of the ways they generously give is by feeding their imposter syndrome with false narratives. The costs of feeding the impostor syndrome include:

- Anxiety and depression
- Perfectionism and workaholism
- Fear of failure leading to risk avoidance
- Reluctance to pursue advancement
- Lack of confidence in abilities
- Diminished satisfaction and fulfillment

Recognize such self-doubting thoughts as baseless stories instead of facts. Then, spend time consciously reframing them into empowering perspectives.

Case Study: A Working Mother Regains Confidence

Jane was an excellent team member for three years. During that time, she was offered a promotion, which she turned down. Jane didn't feel she was ready. A year later, Jane had a child and returned to work. Again, she was offered a promotion, and once again, she turned it down. Jane shared that she wanted to spend more time with her child.

A year later, Jane approached her manager for a promotion at last. She felt ready, and needed to earn more money to improve her family's quality of life. Everyone was happy. All Jane had to do was complete the management assessment, and the job was hers.

When Jane's assessment returned, it showed that she needed more development, even though she was already doing 50 percent of the manager's job effortlessly.

It turned out that Jane was afraid of taking tests. In college, she failed many tests and used extracurricular activities to bolster her GPA. She had a college education, but her belief that she could not do well on tests became a self-fulfilling prophecy.

I wondered if her fear of not being a good mother allowed her inner saboteur to take the assessment in her place. The saboteur was very clever, knowing that management meant more time away from her child.

The results floored Jane and her managers. I oversaw the unit and decided to push her through, and she became a high-performing manager. Within a few months, Jane regained her confidence in her motherhood and the job. Eighteen months after taking the job, she was placed on a fast track to promotion. Her confidence increased, and Jane's talents shone brighter than ever.

Holistic Leaders with high confidence don't think they are better than others. They realize they are valuable in their own unique way and aim to express their gifts without apology.

CHAPTER SIXTEEN

You Cannot Microwave Leadership

"With time and patience, the mulberry
leaf becomes a silk gown."
— Chinese proverb

P atience and persistence are fruitful to the holistic leadership journey. Mastery takes time to fully ripen. This chapter explores embracing the gradual process of learning and growth.

Cultivating true wisdom and character as a leader takes time. In our era of instant downloads and rapid-fire results, practicing patience can seem needless. However, mastery reveals itself through gradually integrating diverse experiences over the years.

I like to think of a Holistic Leader as a just about ripe fruit—not too green, and not overripe. This type of leadership calls for a sturdy foundation, sharpened instincts, bold vision, and swift action. But it all rings hollow if the soul is not yet prepared.

You cannot microwave experience. There are no shortcuts to depth and maturity. But how do you know when your moment to lead ripens?

A leader's readiness shows when she stands on her tiptoes, neither complacent, with both feet flat on the ground nor flapping aimlessly underwater.

My friend Lucy demonstrated this perfectly when she called me for advice about an exciting but daunting new role she was pursuing. While reviewing the job description, Lucy noted three required skills she lacked and asked how to navigate the hiring process and handle those areas.

Instead of fixating on these three gaps as disqualifications, I asked her to focus on the thirteen areas where she already excelled. The missing pieces were just enough to give her a growing edge.

Leading From Your Tiptoes

Too often, women hold themselves back by believing they must completely master every competency before applying for that dream job or promotion. But you cannot speed up to the next level. So, what is the answer?

Women must begin on their tiptoes.

Working on your tiptoes means knowing you don't have all the answers yet, and that's perfectly okay. A Holistic Leader is eager to ask questions, understand different viewpoints, collaborate, and speak honestly when unsure. Wisdom comes not from pretending to know everything, but from recognizing that there is always more to learn. Curiosity is the compass lighting the path ahead. With time and trust, every experience will nourish individual growth.

If your feet are flat on the ground, and you've mastered everything there is to master, then you are in your comfort zone. You are very likely wasting your talents when you see the next step but expect to stay where you are.

On the other side, patience permits progress. When you are not ready, growth is not an edge but a precipice. If this is not your season yet, keep tending your garden. When the time ripens, you will blossom unapologetically. For now, let humility and eagerness feed your continual growth. The tortoise knows the truth—slow and steady cultivates endurance and wisdom.

Three Lessons Leaders Struggle With

Learning from Patience

One of the three lessons I find leaders struggle with is patience. Patience for themselves as well as teaching patience to others. When we try to microwave leadership, something has to give.

A lack of patience hinders visibility, creativity, and the responsibility for growth. Zen Monk Shunryu Suzuki wrote, "In the beginner's mind, there are many possibilities; in the expert's mind, there are few." Don't be in a hurry to arrive. You don't want to lose the precious beginner's growth mentality. It's the season of the foundation of accomplishments. When leaders rush themselves or others, they are trading long-term losses for short-term wins.

Patience allows leaders to stay open and intellectually curious. Patience will give you the precious oxygen you need to push for the finish line and the gold medal.

What area of your career could use a little patience?

Learning from Failure

Another tough lesson many leaders struggle with is learning from failure. Failure is the secret scaffolding that supports eventual success. Rather than avoid or conceal mistakes, truly gifted leaders transparently share their breakdown stories. They extract hard-won wisdom to inspire teams to keep reaching.

When setbacks strike, reflect on missteps without shame; there lies the fertile ground for growth. Dissect what went wrong dispassionately and uncover valuable insights for improvement. Even huge blunders often stem from subtle oversights that can prevent future pitfalls, if identified.

Share your stories of resilience—how you responded to failure with grace, courage, and grit. Shine a light on your struggles, and others will feel less alone. Guide them to take bold risks without the paralyzing fear of imperfection. Well-navigated failure fast-tracks learning and cultivates confidence.

Leaders who conceal mistakes sabotage their team's growth. Like oxygen to a flame, honesty fuels improvement. When people see you stumble, yet bounce back stronger, it liberates them to take chances and learn from their own falls. Breakdowns pave the way for breakthroughs, once lessons take root.

Wear your battle scars proudly, not as badges of shame, but as maps charting paths less traveled. Let your failures become compasses for those who follow behind you; there lies the wisdom that one day may allow them to surpass even your heights.

What failures do you need to display?

Learning from Restoration

In our chaos-fueled era, restless leaders pride themselves on being always *on*. But fierce activity without deliberate restoration depletes our reservoirs of wisdom and vitality. Like athletes, the best leaders carefully program recovery into their routines. The biggest problem is that many leaders perceive their success as the result of overworking. Often, the extended effort is camouflaged with the shield of "hard-working." How can we stop people from doing what they believe led them to where they are?

If they don't learn to practice recovery, their health will pay the price. Often, by the time these leaders are willing to learn to restrain their overwork impulses, their bodies have already been wracked with severe medical conditions.

Before you are forced to slow down, schedule regular breaks—brief moments daily, extended weeks annually—to detach, decompress, and renew your perspective.

Protect relaxation and playtime fiercely. Wholly disengage from work and the world. This means no spiraling emails, texts, or cell phone notifications. You recover exponential amounts of energy when you honor downtime as sacred.

Your stressed mind, exhausted body, and thirsty spirit deserve this replenishing gift too. Leadership is a lifelong journey, along many winding trails of trials, trust, triumphs, and transformations.

We cannot microwave or rush this rich process of becoming a Holistic Leader. You believe you can function with five hours of sleep, but that can't support your best self. Have patience, learn from failure, and give yourself time to restore. The path of leadership holds joy if you travel wisely.

CHAPTER SEVENTEEN

You Can't Teach
Squirrels How to
Cross the Street

*"Each time a woman stands up for herself,
without knowing it possibly, without claiming
it, she stands up for all women."*
— Maya Angelou

W omen leaders often see potential in everyone and seek to nurture growth broadly. But not all deserve your trust or a place on your team. Being overly generous with chances can put your goals and well-being at risk and attract the wrong people to join your team.

You are brilliant. You have many talents. Your heart is in the right place. Now, lead wisely. This chapter will ask you to draw a line defining the space of accountability and opportunity for others and yourself. It will also offer suggestions on exercising discernment in choosing your inner circle, while still leading with an open heart.

See the Good, But Set Boundaries

Viewing others' missteps as opportunities to coach is admirable. However, I've come to realize that many people take advantage of women's inclination to teach patiently and give others endless second chances. While I, too, have received many opportunities and given others too many opportunities when they didn't warrant them, there's a fine line between being patient and being taken for granted.

No matter how well-intentioned, trying to change those who lack motivation, teamwork, and commitment is often an exercise in futility—like teaching squirrels to cross the street safely. You simply cannot teach squirrels to stop at the sidewalk, look both ways and then cross the street when it's clear. Similarly, attempting to instill fundamental values and habits in those unwilling and unable to change themselves mostly creates frustration. It's time to accept people's nature realistically. Although they may be very cute, squirrels don't belong on your team if you're striving for cohesion and progress. No one ever woke up in the morning and said, "I will go to work late, do the minimum as possible, create conflict, break things, take long bathroom breaks, and leave early." But it happens, typically due to a lax work environment and overly agreeable leaders.

No one wants to fire people, but perhaps it's time to reframe the way we view giving notice to people at work. You can teach people the job, but not attitude. If someone doesn't put in effort, doesn't believe in the culture, and doesn't contribute or elevate the environment, they don't belong on your team. You are not penalizing them by letting them go. You are helping them find their nirvana.

Your time is valuable. As a Holistic Leader, you can let them go with grace and compassion. Once you acknowledge that not everyone merits your time and energy, it's easy to make the decision. Statistically, managers spend more time with disengaged people than the top performers. Why would you spend your time with people who are disempowering you? More women than men do just that.

Female leaders are known to give multiple opportunities to people at work. They think of how the lack of a job will impact their families.

THE UMBRELLA EFFECT

Some of us can imagine the children struggling or a landlord evicting them. If this is you, stop it!

I've also seen the delay in exiting people from a team come from fear of confrontation and being judged as the bad boss. Everyone deserves a second chance. However, not everyone should get it on your dime. I've found women being super nice and not addressing major issues for months and years. Then, one day, they've had enough and need to fire someone for something they had been doing for too long, but that was never addressed. This is fear of confrontation.

Avoiding issues costs you more time and aggravation in the long run. You are allowing others to learn a lack of accountability. Soon, you will have more people repeating behaviors you don't want. It then becomes part of the culture. It's easier to correct one individual than a whole bunch of them, and if you take too long to address problems, you will end up needing to change the company's entire culture.

Do yourself a favor and get the squirrels off your team sooner than later. Once you know who the squirrels are, take action.

I find it easier to bite the bullet first thing in the morning when getting people off the team. Leaders typically prefer Thursdays and Fridays to let people go, because it allows employees time over the weekend to process the news and make initial plans, but any day is the right day. Getting people off your team who don't belong there helps them to find greener pastures sooner. Have these conversations with care, respect, and clear expectations. People deserve the opportunity to improve, but if they can't meet reasonable expectations, it's time to pull the plug.

The Power and Curse of Empathy

Women don't want to be called bad bosses. They hesitate to fire squirrels because other people may hate them for letting one of their friends go. However, research has shown that people feel empathy for the fired individual regardless of what they did to get fired. Don't feel trapped by your emotions or the emotions of others around you. Once you know that someone doesn't belong on your team, let them go. This was one of the hardest lessons I had to learn.

I met a leader who told me that everyone he had fired had agreed with him that they should go. He insisted on comprehensive conversations before termination, including an agreement about the actions that would lead to termination. Some people even apologized for letting the leader down.

Always be respectful and act with grace when letting people go. One of my bosses shared great advice that I gauge my behavior with when I have to part ways with an employee. "You will know you let people go with respect and grace if down the road, you see them on the street and they say hello." Let this be your guide.

How to Set Successful Boundaries

Setting healthy boundaries is essential for maintaining balance, preserving mental well-being, and fostering healthy relationships in both personal and professional spheres. Boundaries define the limits of what we are willing to accept and what we consider unacceptable behavior from others. Without clear boundaries, we risk being taken advantage of, overburdened, or disrespected. Establishing successful boundaries requires self-awareness, awareness of your team, clear communication, and the courage to uphold boundaries consistently.

Examine Your Team

1) Your "team" extends beyond direct reporters and those reporting to them. It includes those entrusted with all key aspects of life—doctors, teachers, caregivers, and partners. Choose them carefully.

2) Interview team members thoroughly, and check references to confirm their abilities and ethics. You can review portfolios and shadow them in action. Ask yourself, "Do they walk the talk?"

3) As Stephen Covey says, "Trust takes time, but mistrust happens quickly." Take time to build relationships before fully trusting. Watch for consistency over time.

Right People, Right Roles

1) Match roles to individuals' strengths and interests, not just credentials. A pediatrician may lack adult care experience. An extrovert may struggle at a desk job.

2) Observe people's natural motivations and talents before assigning responsibilities to them. Nurture and elevate natural abilities to accelerate success, morale, and loyalty. If you are doing your job well, you are likely to see potential in them before they see it themselves.

3) Also, continually reassess a person's fit as they grow. Development unlocks new abilities, and passions shift. Adapt roles accordingly.

Address Problems Immediately

1) When left unaddressed, problematic behaviors worsen. Have courageous conversations directly but with compassion.

2) Describe any concerning behavior using facts. Listen to understand their point of view. Find common ground, set expectations, and establish clear boundaries. You must verbalize what you deem unacceptable.

3) If there is no improvement, critique specifics, not the character. Outline the consequences of ongoing issues. Part respectfully if values misalign.

4) Tolerating disrespect, incompetence, or unethical actions erodes the team's culture. Intervene early and decisively to maintain trust and standards.

Cut Ties If Needed

1) Some relationships may become too taxing to sustain. You cannot force people to be happy with what you have to offer. Let them go with love, not anger. Wish them well on their journey, acknowledging that new life lessons await. And be ready to accept imperfect closure.
2) Reflect on learnings from the challenges to strengthen future decisions. How did you ignore the red flags? What boundaries will you uphold moving forward?
3) Devote your energies to new connections. Try not to spend too much time deciphering what happened. If your feelings were hurt, focus ahead, not behind.

The mark of wise Holistic Leadership is elevating relationships that empower while limiting those detrimental to growth. Nurture the worthy and release the harmful. Lead with an open yet discerning heart.

CHAPTER EIGHTEEN

LEADING AS YOUR WHOLE, AUTHENTIC, AND BRILLIANT SELF

*"The journey between what you once were
and who you are now becoming is where
the dance of life really takes place."*
— Barbara DeAngelis

My dear sisters, when you began this book, you set out on a journey of self-discovery and empowerment to become a more confident and authentic Holistic Leader. If you actively applied the strategies in each chapter, you have cultivated mindsets and practices to achieve greater alignment, fulfillment, and impact.

Owning your brilliance requires ongoing courage and belief in your worth. Progress means blazing trails that honor inner truth, even through unexpected twists. Remain guided from within.

You are now equipped to build resonant teams, earn trust through presence, take meaningful steps, and remain true to what matters most.

But this book was not just about professional success. The lessons I've shared facilitate living and leading from the spirit, always.

I hope that reflecting on the knowledge within these pages ignites your inner light to illuminate the path ahead. May you continue leading with abundance, wisdom, and integrated self-trust. Your ripples will expand across communities. This new era requires nothing less than your authentic light and your umbrella.

Thank you for allowing me to share this journey with you. Your brilliance was within you all along. I merely reflected to you what was awaiting discovery, if you dared believe it so.

Owning your radiance is a lifelong process, but your inner spark now glows bright. May it boldly light every step ahead as you become the woman you were destined to be. Our future shines brighter; thanks to you daring to own your gifts fully. Onward in purpose!

I leave you a great poem from one of my favorite authors, Khalil Gibran, "Do Not Love Half Lovers."

Do not love half-lovers
Do not entertain half-friends
Do not indulge in the works of the half-talented
Do not live half a life
and do not die a half death
If you choose silence, then be silent
When you speak, do so until you are finished
Do not silence yourself to say something
And do not speak to be silent
If you accept, then express it bluntly
Do not mask it
If you refuse, then be clear about it
for an ambiguous refusal is but a weak acceptance
Do not accept half a solution
Do not believe half-truths
Do not dream half a dream
Do not fantasize about half-hopes

Half a drink will not quench your thirst
Half a meal will not satiate your hunger
Half the way will get you nowhere
Half an idea will bear you no results
Your other half is not the one you love
It is you in another time yet in the same space
It is you when you are not
Half a life is a life you didn't live,
A word you have not said
A smile you postponed
A love you have not had
A friendship you did not know
To reach and not arrive
Work and not work
Attend only to be absent
What makes you a stranger to them, closest to you
and they are strangers to you
The half is a mere moment of inability
but you are able for you are not half a being
You are a whole that exists to live a life
not half a life

KEY TAKEAWAYS

This conclusion chapter summarizes key lessons and offers final tips to keep strengthening your leadership and staying true to your whole self along the way.

Key Takeaways

- Your uniqueness is a gift - share it confidently
- Double bind expectations are flawed - lead as *you*
- Inner critics obstruct potential - silence them
- Integrate all aspects of self - use your body, mind, and spirit
- Nurture presence and well-being - energy fuels leadership
- Emotional intelligence builds trust and connection
- Purpose and meaning guide fulfilling work
- Master management fundamentals - execution enables vision
- Curate a supportive community - you don't want to do it alone
- Self-efficacy amplifies abilities - believe in your worth
- Values alignment breeds integrity - know what matters most
- Growth takes time and patience - savor the journey
- Discern carefully who to trust - not all deserve entry
- You are *enough* - lead from wholeness

Blaze ahead in your bold brilliance... It's still storming outside, but you've got your umbrella.

WORKS CITED

Ardern, Jacinda. "'Such a Woman Can't Be Prime Minister': New Zealand's Jacinda Ardern Is Doing It Anyway." Vox, 18 May 2020. www.vox. com, https://www.vox.com/first-person/2020/5/18/21262215/jacinda-ardern-new-zealand-prime-minister-coronavirus.

Catalyst. "Women 'Take Care,' Men 'Take Charge': Stereotyping of U.S. Business Leaders Exposed." Catalyst, 5 Oct. 2005. www.catalyst. org, https://www.catalyst.org/research/women-take-care-men-take-charge-stereotyping-of-u-s-business-leaders-exposed/.

Clinton, Hillary Rodham. "It Shouldn't Be Hard to Empathize with Hillary Clinton." Time, 13 Sept. 2017. time.com, https://time.com/4949330/hillary-clinton-what-happened-empathy/.

Cuddy, Amy J. C., et al. "When Professionals Become Mothers, Warmth Doesn't Cut the Ice." Journal of Social Issues, vol. 60, no. 4, 2004, pp. 701–718. https://doi.org/10.1111/j.0022-4537.2004.00381.x..

Eagly, Alice H. "Female Leadership Advantage and Disadvantage: Resolving the Contradictions." Psychology of Women Quarterly, vol. 31, no. 1, 2007, pp. 1–12., https://doi.org/10.1111/j.1471-6402.2007.00326.x.

Eagly, Alice H., and Steven J. Karau. "Role Congruity Theory of Prejudice Toward Female Leaders." Psychological Review, vol. 109, no. 3, 2002, pp. 573–598. https://doi.org/10.1037/0033-295x.109.3.573.

Gimbutas, Marija. The Goddesses and Gods of Old Europe, 6500-3500 BC: Myths, Legends and Cult Images. University of California Press, 2007.

Gino, Francesca, and Caroline Ashley Wilmuth. "Most Leadership Advice Is Useless or Worse." Harvard Business Review, 25 May 2021. hbr.org, https://hbr.org/2021/05/most-leadership-advice-is-useless-or-worse.

Greenleaf, Robert K. "The Servant as Leader." The Robert K. Greenleaf Center, 1991, www.greenleaf.org/what-is-servant-leadership/.

Hackett, Gail, and Nancy E. Betz. "An Exploration of the Mathematics Self-Efficacy/Mathematics Performance Correspondence." Journal for Research in Mathematics Education, vol. 20, no. 3, 1989, pp. 261-273. JSTOR, https://www.jstor.org/stable/749515.

Heilman, Madeline E. "Gender Stereotypes and Workplace Bias." Research in Organizational Behavior, vol. 32, 2012, pp. 113–135. https://doi.org/10.1016/j.riob.2012.11.003.

Ibarra, Herminia, et al. "Women Rising: The Unseen Barriers." Harvard Business Review, Sept. 2013. hbr.org, https://hbr.org/2013/09/women-rising-the-unseen-barriers.

Lopez-Zafra, Esther, et al. "The Effect of Perceived Femininity and Social Support on Psychological Distress in Single Mothers by Choice: The Mediating/Moderating Role of Self-Perceived Success." International Journal of Environmental Research and Public Health, vol. 16, no. 21, 2019. NCBI, https://www.ncbi.nlm.nih.gov/pmc/articles/PMC6861913/.

Matthews, Gail. "Goals Research Summary." Dominican University, 2018. www.dominican.edu, https://www.dominican.edu/academics/lae/undergraduate-programs-1/psych/faculty/assets-gail-matthews/researchsummary2.pdf.

Milkman, Katherine L., et al. "What Happens Before? A Field Experiment Exploring How Pay and Representation Differentially Shape Bias on the Pathway into Organizations." Journal of Applied Psychology, vol. 100, no. 6, 2015, pp. 1678-1712. EBSCOhost, https://doi.org/10.1037/apl0000022.

Northouse, Peter G. Leadership: Theory and Practice. SAGE Publications, 2021.

Okimoto, Tyler G., and Victoria L. Brescoll. "The Price of Power: Power Seeking and Backlash Against Female Politicians." Personality and Social Psychology Bulletin, vol. 36, no. 7, 2010, pp. 923-936. SAGE Journals, https://doi.org/10.1177/0146167210371949.

Sandberg, Sheryl, and Adam Grant. "Speaking While Female." The New York Times, 13 Jan. 2015. www.nytimes.com, https://www.nytimes.com/2015/01/11/opinion/sunday/speaking-while-female.html.

Sandberg, Sheryl, and Nell Scovell. Lean in: Women, Work, and the Will to Lead. W.H. Allen, 2013.

"State of the American Workplace." Gallup.com, Gallup, 2017, https://www.gallup.com/workplace/238085/state-american-workplace-report-2017.aspx.

Schunk & Pajares, 209 p 35 – Self Efficacy

ABOUT THE AUTHOR

With over twenty years of studying Transformational Leadership and self-empowerment, and over thirty years of business experience spanning corporate roles and entrepreneurship, Ana Barreto is a Brazilian-American author, teacher, coach, entrepreneur, and founder of the Body, Mind & Wisdom School for Women, where she aims to help and support women on their journey to self-empowerment.

After obtaining Bachelor's and Master's degrees in Business Administration, Ana was drawn to positive psychology, women's history, spirituality, and Eastern wisdom. While balancing work, family, and education, she voraciously studied these topics, along with leadership, well-being, and unlocking human potential.

In addition to publishing six books on personal growth topics for women, Ana's calling as a guide is to champion the unlimited potential of her readers and students. Having learned what she now writes and teaches, she embodies compassion for the unique pressures and limiting self-perceptions women face as they take on increased responsibilities and leadership roles. She has guided many teams and individuals in the corporate and personal sphere to boldly develop their talents while overcoming fear, imposter syndrome, or avoidance behaviors that can sabotage success.

Ana's purpose is to serve women who need confidence, support, and motivation to enhance their well-being and live to their highest potential. Through writing, teaching, coaching, meditations, and inspirational resources, she guides women to discover their inner brilliance and thrive authentically.

When not writing or empowering women, Ana enjoys cooking, traveling, hiking, biking, kayaking, and spending time with her partner, Jim, their children, family, and friends.